VISIONARY LEADERS OF PURPOSE

Strategies to Unlock Your Destiny

Visionary Author Dr. Tabatha Russell

Table of Contents

Introduction

Visionary Leaders of Purpose: Strategies to Unlock Your Destiny

Leadership is not just a position; it's a purpose. The greatest CEOs of our time are not simply administrators or managers; they are visionaries who see the world not as it is but as it could be. They lead with clarity, conviction, and a relentless drive to turn their bold ideas into lasting legacies. These leaders understand that success isn't just measured in revenue or market share but, in the impact they create, the people they inspire, and the lives they transform.

Visionary Leaders of Purpose was born out of a desire to highlight the strategies, principles, and mindsets of the world's most impactful leaders, those who embody not just success but significance. This book brings together an extraordinary group of CEOs, each of whom has carved out a unique path to leadership. They have faced challenges, made pivotal decisions, and embraced innovative strategies that have not only shaped their organizations but, also influenced entire industries.

This is not a typical book on leadership. You won't find generic advice or one-size-fits-all solutions here. Instead, you will discover real stories, hard-won lessons, and actionable strategies from leaders who have been in the trenches and emerged with the kind of wisdom that only comes from experience. These are leaders who have dared to think differently, act courageously, and align their decisions with a deeper sense of purpose.

In the chapters ahead, you'll hear directly from CEOs who lead with vision and heart. They will share how they navigated the complexities of scaling a business, pivoted in the face of uncertainty, and built teams that thrive in even the most challenging environments. You'll learn about their guiding principles, innovative frameworks, and the personal philosophies that have defined their leadership journeys.

This book is for aspiring leaders, seasoned executives, and anyone who seeks to understand what it truly means to lead with purpose. Whether you're leading a Fortune 500 company, a start-up, or a small team, the insights in these pages will challenge you to think bigger, act with greater intention, and lead in a way that leaves a meaningful legacy.

Visionary Leaders of Purpose is not just a collection of stories; it's a roadmap for those who aspire to lead with impact. By the end of this book, you'll have a clearer understanding of what it takes to stand out as a visionary leader and practical tools you can apply in your own journey. More importantly, you'll be inspired to lead not just for profit, but for purpose.

Welcome to a community of extraordinary leaders who are shaping the future. Let their stories ignite your imagination and empower you to chart your own path as a **Visionary Leader of Purpose.**

Let's begin.

Dr. Tabatha Russell

International Keynote Speaker | Best-Selling Author | Financial Expert | Investor

Change your life through mastering your vision and your voice."

– Dr. Tabatha Russell

Dr. Tabatha Russell, affectionately known as the "Money Makeover Mogul," is a highly sought-after speaker, best-selling author, and financial expert. With over 20 years of experience, she empowers corporate and collegiate audiences to redefine their relationship with money, unlocking financial freedom, stability, and independence.

Her mission is to guide individuals, from employees to CEOs, of their own lives, businesses, and legacies. Dr. Tabatha's dynamic and transformational keynotes have captivated audiences at major events, including the Leadership Experience Tour and Sisterhood Global Conference.

As the founder of Next, Level CEO Mastermind, Breakthrough Millionaires Academy, and Inside Inspired

Women LLC™, Dr. Tabatha equips high-achieving business owners with strategies to elevate their businesses and create multiple income streams. She is the author of *I Divorced My Money and Married My Mindset*, a best-selling financial guide designed to challenge traditional money beliefs.

Recognized for her leadership and impact, Dr. Tabatha has received three doctoral degrees and has been featured on platforms like ABC, NBC, FOX, and CBS, as well as in magazines such as Speakers Magazine, TapIn Magazine and Shoutout Atlanta.

Connect on website at: DrTabathaRussell.com

Chapter 1: The Voice of Purpose: Using Your Unique Voice to Impact the World

Dr. Tabatha Russell

There are moments in life that shift everything, moments when you feel the borders of your comfort zone stretching and sense the weight of something extraordinary just beyond the horizon. For me, that moment came during a seemingly ordinary speaking engagement. I was invited to deliver a workshop on financial empowerment for a small audience. I stepped onto the stage, clutching my notes, and felt the familiar nerves that always accompanied speaking in front of a crowd. But as I began to speak, something shifted.

The room was silent, not the kind of silence that comes from disinterest, but the kind that signals full, undivided attention. People weren't just listening; they were leaning in, nodding, and scribbling notes furiously. I saw tears well up in someone's eyes as I shared how I had "**Divorced my Money and Married My Mindset**," a decision that had set me on a path toward financial freedom and purpose. Who knew the title of my best-selling book would be a launching pad for something amazing? The room erupted in applause when I finished, and a line formed. Person after person came up to tell me how my words had unlocked something in them with hope, clarity, and courage.

That night, I sat in my car, overwhelmed by the realization that this was no longer just a job or a passion. This was my purpose. I was on the verge of something big, and the only way to fully step into it was to expand my borders and invest in mastering the gift I had been given by using my voice to impact others.

I didn't know all the answers, but I knew one thing: my voice had power. And so does yours.

The Voice of Purpose

Being the Voice of Purpose isn't about being the loudest person in the room. It's about aligning your unique gift with your message and delivering it in a way that transforms lives. Your voice is the channel through which your purpose flows. Whether you're an entrepreneur, a leader, a coach, or a creative, your voice has the potential to inspire change, heal wounds, and open doors for others.

Your voice doesn't have to compete with the noise around you. Instead, it must stand apart, grounded in authenticity and fueled by a clear understanding of the gift only you can offer. Consider this: the world isn't looking for another carbon copy of someone else's success story. The world needs *your* story, *your* perspective, and *your* solutions. There's an unmatched power in embracing the uniqueness of your voice because it allows you to connect with people in ways that no one else can.

Think about the people you've admired throughout your life. Chances are, it wasn't their volume or charisma alone that inspired you, it was their ability to speak directly to your heart. Purposeful voices don't merely inform; they ignite something within us. They challenge us to think differently, to believe in ourselves, and to take bold action. But those voices didn't magically appear overnight. They were cultivated, sharpened, and refined through self-awareness and intentional practice.

Being the Voice of Purpose also means recognizing that your voice is not just about *you*. It's about the people you're called to serve. It's about identifying the pain points, desires, and dreams of your audience and meeting them where they are. Purposeful voices have a way of making others feel seen, heard, and valued. They empower others to believe in possibilities they hadn't yet imagined for themselves.

Yet, aligning your voice with your purpose can feel intimidating. You may wonder if your story is "good enough" or question whether your message will truly resonate. Let me assure you: your story, with all its highs and lows, is precisely what someone needs to hear. Your voice becomes purposeful not because it's perfect, but because it's honest, vulnerable, and deeply connected to your gift.

But here's the truth: realizing this potential doesn't happen by accident. It requires intentionality, skill, and the courage to step into uncharted territory. In this chapter, we'll explore the three key skills that will help you align your voice with your purpose and deliver real results:

1. **Authentic Self-Awareness**
2. **Strategic Communication**
3. **Purposeful Execution**

Let's break these down and equip you with practical tools to step into your purpose boldly and unapologetically.

Skill 1: Authentic Self-Awareness

Before you can impact others, you must first understand yourself. Authentic self-awareness is the foundation of becoming the Voice of Purpose. It's about uncovering who you truly are, what you stand for, and how your experiences shape your unique gift.

My Journey of Self-Awareness

After that transformative speaking engagement, I realized I needed to deepen my understanding of what made my voice resonate with others. I began to reflect on my life's journey, not just the successes but the challenges and turning points that had shaped me. I asked myself hard questions:

- What lessons have my struggles taught me?
- What excites me so much that I lose track of time when I'm doing it?
- What are the patterns in my life that reveal my deepest passions and strengths?

The answers were clear. I am passionate about helping others break free from the chains of scarcity, financial woes, emotional stress, and mental challenges, and step into abundance. But to communicate effectively, I needed to embrace every aspect of me, not just the polished, professional version. People resonated with my story because it was real.

How You Can Cultivate Authentic Self-Awareness

1. **Reflect on Your Journey:**
   Spend time journaling about the pivotal moments in your life. What challenges have you overcome? What gifts emerged from those challenges?
2. **Identify Your Core Values:**
   Your values are the compass that guides your voice.

List the top five values that matter most to you and consider how they show up in your message.

3. **Embrace Your Authenticity:**
Vulnerability is your greatest strength. Don't be afraid to share your imperfections, they make your voice relatable and real.

Practical Steps to Implement:

- Start a journal specifically for self-reflection. Write about your wins, your fears, and the lessons you've learned.
- Create a "life map" that outlines your key events, decisions, and milestones in your journey. Look for patterns that reveal your purpose.
- Practice self-awareness exercises, like mindfulness or working with a mentor who can offer perspective.

Skill 2: Strategic Communication

Once you know your purpose, the next step is learning how to communicate it effectively. Strategic communication ensures your unique voice doesn't just make noise; it creates impact.

My Experience with Strategic Communication

After deciding to invest in my voice, I knew I had to refine how I delivered my message. I attended workshops on storytelling, studied world-class speakers, and practiced relentlessly. I crafted a signature message that aligned with my purpose: helping others break financial chains and step into abundance. I learned how to tailor my message to different audiences, whether it was a conference of CEOs or in the classroom training world-class leaders around the country.

One of the biggest lessons I learned during this journey was that delivery is just as important as content. Even the most powerful message can fall flat if it isn't communicated with conviction, emotion, and relevance. I began to focus on how I showed up, not just physically but energetically. Was I speaking with passion? Did my words convey the urgency and hope my audience needed to feel? These questions forced me to step out of my comfort zone and continuously improve my approach.

Another game-changer was understanding the importance of listening as part of communication. As a speaker, it's easy to focus solely on what you want to say, but the most impactful voices are the ones that reflect the needs and desires of the audience. I started to engage more deeply with those I served, asking questions, seeking feedback, and paying close attention to their struggles and aspirations. This allowed me to refine my message and how I delivered it, ensuring it resonated.

Tailoring my message also requires adaptability. Speaking to a room full of CEOs requires a different tone and focus than working with young professionals starting their careers. I learned to adjust my language, examples, and delivery style without compromising my message's core. This ability to adapt ensured that my voice could reach diverse audiences while remaining authentic to my purpose.

The result? My message began to resonate more deeply. I went from being a speaker to being *the* speaker people remembered long after the event ended. What surprised me most wasn't just the accolades or the invitations to return, it was the personal stories people shared with me afterward.

They told me how my words inspired them to take a leap, break a cycle, or begin a transformation they had avoided for years. That's when I knew my voice wasn't just a tool but a bridge to empowerment for others.

Master Strategic Communication

1. **Clarify Your Message:**
   What is the one thing you want people to take away from your voice? Your message should be concise, compelling, and aligned with your purpose.
2. **Adapt to Your Audience:**
   Different audiences have different needs. Learn to tailor your message while staying true to your core values.
3. **Use Storytelling:**
   Stories are the most powerful way to communicate your purpose. Share stories that illustrate your message and connect emotionally with your audience.

Practical Steps to Implement:

- Develop a "message map" that outlines your core message and how it can be adapted for different platforms (speaking, social media, etc.).
- Record yourself, practice your message and review it to identify areas for improvement.
- Attend workshops or hire a coach to hone your storytelling and presentation skills.

Skill 3: Purposeful Execution

A strong voice without action is like a song that's never sung. Purposeful execution is where your voice turns into tangible results.

My Journey of Purposeful Execution

A strong voice without action is like a song that's never been sung, beautiful in potential but never realized. It carries the promise of impact, yet without the courage and intention to bring it to life, it remains silent, unheard, and ultimately unfulfilled. Purposeful execution is the bridge between what could be and what is. It's where your voice moves beyond ideas and inspiration to create tangible, lasting results that not only transform your own life but also ripple outward to impact others.

This is where the real work begins. It's not enough to know your purpose or even to articulate it powerfully. True purpose demands action. It asks you to step into the arena, take risks, and commit to doing the necessary work to bring your vision into reality. Purposeful execution challenges you to align your words with your actions and to show up consistently, even when progress feels slow or obstacles arise.

The beauty of purposeful execution lies in its ability to create momentum. With each intentional step, your voice grows stronger, your message reaches further, and your confidence builds. This is where the magic happens—not in grand, sweeping gestures, but in the daily, deliberate choices that bring your purpose to life.

Make no mistake: execution is not about perfection. It's about persistence. It's about being willing to adjust your approach, learn from your experiences, and keep moving forward even when the path ahead is unclear. Purposeful execution requires a mindset of growth and resilience, reminding yourself that every effort you make is part of a greater picture.

Purpose without execution is like a melody that never escapes the confines of your mind. When you pair your voice with action, you give your purpose the space to breathe, evolve, and ultimately transform the world around you.

How You Can Execute Purposefully

1. **Set Specific Goals:**
   Define what success looks like for your voice. Break these goals into smaller, actionable steps.
2. **Create a System:**
   Purposeful execution requires organization. Use tools like planners, apps, or accountability groups to stay on track.
3. **Measure Your Impact:**
   Regularly evaluate the effectiveness of your voice. Are you reaching the people you want to reach? Are you creating the change you envision?

Practical Steps to Implement:

- Write down three big goals for the next six months. Break them into smaller weekly tasks.
- Schedule daily time to work on amplifying your voice, whether creating content, practicing speaking, or networking.
- Track your progress and celebrate small wins to stay motivated.

Step Into Your Purpose

Your voice has the power to transform lives. It's time to stop playing small and start stepping into the fullness of your purpose.

If you're ready to amplify your voice and align it with your unique gift, I invite you to a **free discovery session**. Together, we'll identify your unique strengths, clarify your message, and create a lasting impact strategy.

Contact Information:

- **Website: www.tabatharussell.com**
- **Email: support@DrTabathaRussell.com**

Remember, the world is waiting for what only you can offer. Step into your purpose today.

Conclusion

Being the Voice of Purpose means embracing your unique gift, communicating it strategically, and taking purposeful action. By cultivating authentic self-awareness, refining your communication, and executing with intention, you can align your voice with your purpose and create a lasting impact.

Don't wait for the "perfect moment." The world needs your voice now.

Dr. LeTasha S. Robinson-Coleman

Dr. LeTasha S. Robinson-Coleman is what many would call a survivor. At eighteen months she was left at the Department of Social Services and placed inside the system. Having survived physical, emotional, and sexual abuse, Dr. LeTasha continues to survive.

Dr. LeTasha, with an undiagnosed learning disability, had a passion for reading but faced challenges in school. Despite being in fifth grade and reading at a second/third-grade level, a turning point came when a teacher took a chance and placed LeTasha at the same reading level as her peers. This moment ignited a spark of hope within her, leading to a lifetime of academic accomplishments.

Achievements include graduating high school with honors, completing a Marketing degree with minors in Mathematics and Accounting from Benedict College, earning an MBA from Strayer University, and most recently, obtaining a Doctorate in Christian Counseling from Glory to Glory School of Theology.

Her journey and survival did not stop there; she fought breast cancer in 2020 and is now in remission. Dr. Robinson-Coleman serves as a motivator, guiding individuals to unlock their potential when faced with life's challenges. Maintaining motivation during uncertain times is essential, and her teachings and motivational messages have empowered numerous individuals. Additionally, she is an accomplished published author and playwright.

Chapter 2: From Disqualified to Qualified: Reclaiming Your Narrative

Dr. Letasha Robinson Coleman

At thirty-eight years old, I found myself gazing at an unused passport on the brink of expiration and a symbol of how fear had dominated my life. Although I called myself a woman of faith, I realized my belief mainly rested on what I could do alone.

Growing up in foster care, enduring poverty, and coping with abandonment taught me not to expect much from life. My idea of "contentment" became a shield against further hurt. I made many decisions out of fear, and the ones I avoided were also due to fear. Before I knew it, I was living in an "open-door jail cell" of my own making, feeling trapped without recognizing how I ended up there.

Unpacking the Past

My thirty-eight years were riddled with trauma: sexual abuse, domestic violence, homelessness, the list goes on. Life had taught me to expect nothing. I vividly recall buying juice once and hearing fear whisper, *"What if you can't afford more? Don't drink it all."* When I finally wanted more, I discovered it had expired two months earlier, a stark reminder that missed opportunities can spoil if we never seize them.

Unlike baseball, where you run to first base even after a strikeout, life offers no guarantees. If you miss an opportunity, it may never return. Yet, I invite you on a journey of self-discovery that freed me from fear and led me to write books, create plays, and discover deeper purpose. My life with its struggles, tears, joys, and sorrows, is my story. Join me in witnessing how God can truly turn ashes into beauty.

The Start of the Lie

When I was eight, my foster mother stormed outside, angry at something I'd done. Her words changed my life forever:

"I'm calling DSS to come take you away. Your mother didn't want you, and neither do I."

Those words have echoed through my mind for forty-three years. Even as a child, I never fully understood why I felt alone in a crowded room. Family gatherings left me feeling mocked or ignored, especially because my skin was darker than my siblings'. The truth was unmistakable: I was a foster child, different in ways that became painfully obvious.

My mother fostered many children, so it wasn't unusual for strangers to appear with their belongings in black trash bags at any hour. I never dreamed I might join their ranks, until one day of anger taught me that I, too, could be sent away.

Overcommitment and Conditional Love

After that threatening day, I sat on a couch for hours, waiting for DSS to come. It never happened, but my foster mother's cold shoulder continued. I did everything I could to make her talk to me; only when she needed something done, would she finally speak. From then on, I believed I had to be "needed" to be valued. My worth depended on how much time, money, or gifts that I could give to keep people around.

At sixteen, I secretly found my birth mother, convinced she had given me up out of love. Her words, *"No, I simply didn't want you"*, confirmed my worst fears. It wasn't my teenage self, listening to those words, but the eight-year-old who still clung to hopes and dreams. Even at thirty-eight, I wrestled with that child's unresolved pain, trying to please anyone who came into my life, so I'd feel "needed." When I ran out of ways to help others, I questioned my worth, not so much with them, but within myself.

My dysfunctional need to make my foster mother happy set a damaging pattern in my life, influencing my future relationships. I was sure love was out of my reach. When my birth mother repeated that she hadn't wanted me, I tried to buy her approval. At sixteen, I used my small earnings to give her money. While I was giving, she seemed content; once I stopped, her affection disappeared.

Finding Purpose in Pain

Years passed with this mindset until I had a breakthrough. I was asked to speak to a young adult who had dropped out of high school. Standing before them, I felt their skepticism, *"Who is she, and what can she offer?"* But when I told my story, many were moved to tears. I reminded them that life doesn't have dead ends; it has moments when we choose to give up. They realized they could still stand up and keep moving forward.

I saw myself reflected in their eyes. Like the difference between a lottery winner and a self-made millionaire, a person with lived experiences can rebuild after loss, while someone who relies on luck can't replicate success without another stroke of fortune. Many of us don't appreciate how priceless our unique stories are. No one else can be you, and no one else can succeed at being you. That same past you might be ashamed of is exactly what God can use to transform others.

Passport from a Disqualified Life to a Qualified Life

I want to share five principles that can help you move from feeling disqualified to recognizing you are qualified. Your struggles haven't been just for you; they serve as a living witness that God remains in control.

"And Jesus said to him, 'See that you tell no one; but go your way, show yourself to the priest, and offer the gift that Moses commanded, as a testimony to them.'"

Matthew 8:4 (NKJV)

1. Guard Your Testimony

Jesus instructed the healed man not to speak of it yet. We often tell our stories too soon, confiding in people who aren't equipped to guide us and may encourage our bad choices. Before sharing your testimony widely, ensure you've taken the initial steps toward real transformation.

2. Seek Spiritual Examination

Jesus said, *"Show yourself to the priest."* After overcoming hardship, resist the urge to immediately broadcast your experience. Allow a trusted mentor or spiritual leader to assess your progress and guide you.

3. Embrace Spiritual Covering

Submitting to spiritual guidance can be misunderstood, but it's a form of protection and growth. Pruning and refining make you stronger. Far from limiting your freedom, wise counsel elevates you to your next level.

4. Continue in Generosity

Like an open water faucet that flows freely, blessings continue only when you remain generous. The moment you shut yourself off, the blessings cease.

5. Share Your Story

Finally, once your healing is secure, God will position you to help those who need encouragement. Your past can become a platform for others to value their own experiences.

When Life Truly Begins

We don't know when life "begins" for us personally. For me, it started in the womb. My birth mother didn't want another daughter and resented her pregnancy. She chose a life of prostitution, and only sought prenatal care to avoid jail.

Though I could delve further into that story, I'd rather emphasize this truth: life truly begins the moment you decide to live in spite of obstacles. Your beginnings don't define your ending, only *you* can decide that. Now is the time to transition from a life you believe disqualifies you to one in which you realize you're fully qualified. Think of this as your **Passport**; the question is, what stamps will you collect on your journey?

Stay Connected:

Email: Lsrobins@yahoo.com

Facebook: LeTasha S. Coleman

Instagram: Lsrobins

Payhip: https://payhip.com/LeTashaSColeman

Dr. Acetra "Dee" Russell

Dr. Acetra "Dee" Russell is a dynamic leader, devoted wife to Anthony Russell, and proud mother of a blended family. She is both a Business Integrator with a Fortune 500 company and a passionate healing coach dedicated to helping others find resilience and purpose.

As the author of "100% Healed: A Mother's Journey of Moving Mountains to Heal the Heart after Death and Divorce" and the Founder of Moving Mountain Ministries, Dr. Russell inspires women to navigate life's challenges with grace and strength. She also co-leads A&M FaithFusion, empowering individuals through faith-based coaching and conferences.

Known as the "Passionate Healer of the Heart," Dr. Russell is driven by her vision to unite women through shared testimonies and revelations. Her mission is to guide others toward healing and resilience, believing that her story of overcoming grief and adversity can inspire people of all ages, nationalities, statuses, and beliefs.

Chapter 3: Resilience: Rising from the Ashes

Dr. Acetra Dee Russell

Resilience is often described as the ability to recover quickly from adversity to withstand challenges and bounce back from life's most difficult events. For me, resilience became a lifeline, an unexpected strength anchored in faith. I discovered this quality only after a tragedy that changed my family's life forever.

Facing the Unthinkable

In 2007, our lives were irrevocably changed when my ex-husband (then husband) and I received devastating news: our youngest daughter had been diagnosed with an astrocytoma glioma brain tumor, a condition with a survival rate of less than 2%. The thought of our seven-year-old undergoing multiple surgeries, chemotherapy, and radiation was so heartbreaking. Each day felt like a new battle as we watched her suffer. My prayers became more intense; I clung to my faith, though at times it felt fragile. Journaling served as my outlet; it became my way to cope with the overwhelming wave of emotions.

Despite our hopes, in 2009, we lost our precious daughter. It felt as though the world had ended. The grief was overwhelming, and I struggled to imagine a life without her. Six months later, my 16-year marriage ended too. Our relationship had been strained before our daughter's illness, and her passing only magnified the distance and brokenness caused by infidelity and deception. Suddenly, I was a single mother of one instead of a married mother of two, left questioning an uncertain future.

Grief, Struggle, and a Shattered Heart

Losing a child inflicts unimaginable pain. I cycled through guilt, confusion, and deep sadness for years. At times, I wanted only to sleep, numbing my anguish with prescription medication, which was only a fleeting bandage for a wound too profound to be healed by pills. Yet I realized I had another child who needed me, and I could not allow grief to fully consume me.

Anger surfaced as well. I questioned why God would allow me to bring a beautiful soul into this world, only to take her away before she could grow into the remarkable woman I envisioned. This was a painful chapter in my faith journey, learning to trust and grapple with loss all at once.

Healing proved a slow, painstaking process. It began with small steps by attending therapy, sharing my daughter's story, and finding solace in my faith. Journaling became a lifeline, a safe space to release my grief in a constructive way. Each modest milestone represented a victory, a testament to a resilience I hadn't realized was possible.

Determined to Thrive

My drive to survive and heal ignited a fierce resolve to return to school, earning the credentials I needed to guide other women toward resilience and triumph over tragedy. I learned that it was okay not to be okay, to grieve deeply, but not to remain in that despair. This revelation led me to establish **Moving Mountains Ministries**; a platform devoted to helping women pursue personal and emotional wholeness. To me, resilience means refusing to surrender, both for myself and for the women I serve through this ministry.

Building Resilience: Key Strategies

Through my own experience, I discovered vital steps that allowed me to rebuild my life and thrive in the face of adversity. These same principles form the core of the support we offer at Moving Mountains Ministries:

1. **Seeking Support**
   Lean on loved ones, family, friends, and mentors who can provide solace, guidance, and a listening ear. A strong support network ensures you are not alone and can offer tangible help or emotional comfort when life becomes overwhelming.
2. **Embracing Faith**
   Faith serves as a foundation, offering strength and hope when despair seems insurmountable. For me, turning to God brought a sense of continuity and a steadfast reminder that healing was possible. My relationship with God anchored me and gave me the courage to move forward.
3. **Engaging in Therapy**
   Therapy provides a confidential space to unpack grief, trauma, and emotional struggles. Talking openly with a professional allowed me to process pain and uncertainty, teaching me coping strategies essential for rebuilding. Therapy became one of the most vital pieces of my healing puzzle.
4. **Journaling**
   Writing down thoughts, feelings, and experiences can bring clarity and relief. During my daughter's hospitalization, journaling served as both a record

of medical updates and an outlet for my emotions. It also became a tangible way to see my progress over time.

5. **Taking Small Steps**
   Set manageable goals, focusing on incremental progress rather than monumental change. For me, sharing my story was a pivotal first step. Later, pursuing further education equipped me to better support and uplift others in their time of need.
6. **Giving Back**
   True resilience involves channeling your strength into helping others. By founding Moving Mountains Ministries, I turned my personal pain into a legacy of support and inspiration for those navigating similar hardships.
7. **Continuing Learning and Growth**
   Embracing ongoing personal and professional development keeps you adaptable in a constantly evolving world. Going back to school taught me skills vital for coaching women, allowing me to broaden my impact and become an effective guide in their healing.
8. **Acceptance and Resilience**
   Acceptance acknowledges present challenges without surrendering to them. Resilience emerges from confronting obstacles head-on, transforming pain into growth. I accepted that it was okay to grieve, to be angry, and not to have all the answers, but I chose to keep moving forward.

Additional Keys to Strength and Healing

1. **Embracing Change and Adaptability**
   Life's unpredictability demands a willingness to adjust and evolve. Embracing change after my

daughter's loss and divorce meant redefining my identity, redefining success, and opening myself to new possibilities.

2. **Practicing Gratitude**
   Even amidst hardship, focusing on the blessings no matter how small, cultivates a resilient mindset. Gratefulness keeps hope alive and helps you see the path forward, even in darkness.

Moving Mountains Ministries: A Mission of Hope

Over time, I learned that resilience isn't innate, it's a response born from adversity. It's the power to rebuild from life's rubble and to honor those we've lost by living in a way that would make them proud. My surviving daughter needed a strong role model; a mother who stood for endurance and determination.

Through resilience, I embraced faith, leaned on supportive loved ones, and sought professional help. Journaling became a safe harbor, while going back to school gave me the knowledge to uplift others through my mission. Founding **Moving Mountains Ministries** has been a profound way to transform my own journey into a source of hope for others. We host workshops, tea parties, and community events to create spaces where women can share experiences and grow stronger together.

If you or someone you know needs guidance, please visit my website at **acetrarussell.com.** Together, let's move mountains.

A Final Word on Resilience

By sharing my story and the steps I took to foster resilience, I hope to encourage and empower you to face your challenges with courage and hope. Resilience isn't about never stumbling; it's about getting up every time you fall. It's about discovering your capacity to endure hardship and become stronger on the other side.

Whatever you may be confronting, grief, loss, or any major challenge in life, remember that you have the power to heal. Lean on your network, ground yourself in faith, consult professionals when needed, and take small steps toward meaningful goals. With patience and unwavering resolve, you too can move mountains.

Dr. Jacqueline Dowdy

As the CEO and President of Vision in Action Business Solutions based in Durham, NC, I, **Dr. Jacqueline Dowdy**, am dedicated to realizing the potential of entrepreneurial spirits and organizations. My commitment lies in cultivating innovative and strategic pathways tailored to the distinctive needs of each individual, entrepreneur, small business, non-profit, university, or large enterprise seeking our services. With an extensive background in leadership development and organizational management, I steer our mission to envision and implement practical solutions that foster growth, performance, and operational excellence.

Under my leadership, **Vision in Action Business Solutions** has blossomed into a haven for those looking to enhance their leadership acumen or amplify their team dynamics. My team and I thrive on the transformation that ensues when structured guidance blends with our clients' unique visions. We take pride in being active partners in their journey, whether it's for crafting actionable strategies, navigating transformational changes, or refining business processes to align with their overarching goals. Our client's success is our utmost satisfaction, and together, we embark on a collaborative venture toward achieving remarkable results.

Her dedication to faith-based leadership led her to work extensively with churches, pastors, and community leaders in various regions, including Africa, Florida, North Carolina, and Georgia. Through her ministry and professional endeavors, Dr. Jacqueline exemplifies how faith can be a powerful catalyst for social transformation, motivating others to pursue a shared vision of justice, equity, and compassion.

Educated at esteemed institutions such as Elon University and Florida A&M University, Dr. Jacqueline holds Accounting, Divinity, and Business Administration degrees, providing a solid foundation for her multifaceted career. She further enhanced her expertise with certificates in Nonprofit Management from Duke University and Executive Leadership from Cornell University, reflecting her dedication to staying at the forefront of best practices in her field. Her academic journey culminated in a PhD in Educational Leadership from Florida A&M University, underscoring her commitment to continual learning and scholarly distinction. This diverse and rigorous academic background equips Dr. Jacqueline with the knowledge and skills to excel in various leadership roles and effectively guide others. Her education and extensive professional experience position her as a thought leader and trusted advisor in ministry and the nonprofit and business sectors.

Chapter 4: Turn Deficits, Delays, and Deceptions into Triumphs

Dr Jacqueline Dowdy

Throughout my career in administrative and executive roles, I have encountered many challenges that have profoundly shaped my understanding of effective leadership. My professional journey has often led me into the heart of organizations grappling with severe issues: financial instability, compromised licensure and accreditation, and pervasive toxic culture. These experiences have tested my leadership and provided me with the drive to write D^3 Leadership Blueprint: Turning Deficits, Delays, and Deception into Triumphs. During a challenging time in leadership, I had to decide to make a change in my life. As a leader, transitions are necessary to rethink and reposition yourself. What I have discovered in this process is that I had been putting my dreams and vision for my life on hold. Don't get me wrong, having a job was necessary to live and make ends meet. However, in the thick of disruptions, distractions, and deception, I realized it was time to shift. A move towards my dreams and desires for my life.

I recognize that my professional leadership journey was all to prepare me for such a time as this. To be honest, I was spiritually broken, mentally and physically exhausted. The truth is that God had spoken to me a year before to leave my then-present position as CEO, but I talked myself into staying. The mistake we often make is trying to prove something to ourselves and others. What I learned is that it doesn't matter! You must listen to the Holy Spirit and obey. Moreover, you must be conscious of your well-being mentally, physically, and spiritually. Although it was obvious that the organization was dealing with recurring issues of deficits, delays, and deception in all areas, the staff didn't know all the nuances that happened behind the scenes. I didn't want the agency to fail because it was too critical to the community and vital for the people it served daily. I won't go deep into the details but sprinkle information throughout to testify to my experience.

In several roles, I faced organizations struggling with financial troubles. These financial deficits were more than just numbers on a balance sheet; they represented a lack of cash reserves that jeopardized the continuity of essential programs and services. The struggle to keep operations afloat amidst dwindling resources was a daily battle, compounded by a lack of board support and engagement. This absence of backing from the board undermined strategic efforts and intensified the sense of isolation and frustration.

Compounding these financial difficulties were issues with licensure and/or accreditation. Navigating these bureaucratic hurdles was a relentless challenge, often exacerbated by a toxic organizational culture. The work environment was characterized by deceitful team leaders and a general erosion of trust, which created an atmosphere where transparency was scarce and ethical standards were compromised. Hiring the right people in such an environment was another formidable challenge. Finding and retaining staff who were both skilled and aligned with the organization's values was an uphill battle. High staff turnover further destabilized the organization, leading to a continual cycle of disruption and uncertainty.

The impact of these challenges on my physical and mental health was significant. Leading in a toxic environment, dealing with deceptive practices, and managing the stress of financial and operational instability took a toll on my well-being. The relentless pressure to address these issues while maintaining morale and delivering results was exhausting and often overwhelming.

Through these experiences, the **D³ Leadership Blueprint** and **Vision in Action Business Solutions** (VIABS), LLC was born. The blueprint is a theoretical construct, and a practical tool forged from real-world experiences. It emerged as a response to the deficits, delays, and deceptions I encountered. It became a framework to address these challenges head-on, drawing from the lessons learned in the trenches. By systematically tackling deficits in resources and capabilities, managing the inevitable delays with strategic foresight, and combating deception with integrity and transparency, the D³ Leadership Blueprint aims to provide a comprehensive approach to leadership that fosters resilience, ethical practices, and sustainable success. It represents a commitment to transforming leadership challenges into opportunities for growth and improvement, grounded in strategic insight and personal resilience.

D³ Leadership Blueprint: Turning Deficits, Delays, and Deceptions into Triumphs

For established businesses, start-ups, non-profits, and personal development, the D³ Leadership Blueprint provides actionable insights for enhancing leadership effectiveness. It helps organizations address key challenges, build stronger teams, and align personal and professional growth with ethical values, making it a valuable tool for diverse leadership contexts.

The D³ Leadership Blueprint is a comprehensive framework designed to enhance leadership effectiveness by addressing three critical challenges: deficits, delays, and deception.

Leadership is a cornerstone of any successful organization, guiding vision, strategy, and culture while shaping the ethical and moral framework of the business. In today's dynamic and often unpredictable marketplace, leaders face significant obstacles that can undermine their ability to drive organizational success. The D^3 Leadership Blueprint provides practical strategies and biblical wisdom to navigate these challenges, fostering growth, resilience, and ethical integrity in both personal and professional realms. For more information and to register for the D^3 Leadership Masterclass, visit our website and contact us at: **www.drjacquelinedowdy.com**.

Core Principles of the D^3 Leadership Blueprint

The D^3 Leadership Blueprint is grounded in three core principles: addressing deficits, managing delays, and combating deception. Each principle offers practical strategies and insights for enhancing leadership effectiveness and organizational resilience.

1. Addressing Deficits

Deficits in leadership refer to gaps in resources, skills, or character that hinder an organization's ability to achieve its goals. These deficits can manifest as financial shortfalls, lack of expertise, or deficiencies in leadership qualities such as integrity or vision. Addressing these deficits is crucial for maintaining operational efficiency and organizational health.

The blueprint advocates for conducting thorough assessments of an organization's current state, including evaluating financial performance, team capabilities, and leadership practices. By pinpointing specific areas of shortfall, leaders can develop targeted strategies to address these issues effectively. Effective resource management, continuous learning, and a commitment to ethical behavior are key to addressing deficits.

2. Managing Delays

Delays are inevitable in business and can arise from various factors, such as unforeseen circumstances, bureaucratic hurdles, or external disruptions. While delays are a natural part of the business process, how leaders manage them can significantly impact organizational performance and morale.

The blueprint emphasizes the importance of strategic foresight and flexibility in managing delays. Leaders should develop contingency plans, prioritize critical tasks, and communicate transparently with stakeholders to mitigate the impact of delays on organizational goals.

3. Combating Deception

Deception in business undermines trust and damages organizational integrity. It can manifest as dishonesty, unethical practices, or manipulation of facts. Addressing deception is critical for maintaining a positive organizational culture and protecting the organization's reputation.

The blueprint advocates for a commitment to integrity and transparency. Leaders should model ethical behavior, promote a culture of honesty, and implement systems for monitoring and addressing deceptive practices.

Application of the D^3 Leadership Blueprint

For Established Businesses

For established businesses, addressing deficits involves proactively identifying and overcoming gaps. The D^3

Leadership Blueprint offers valuable strategies for assessing organizational performance, managing resources effectively, and investing in professional development. Leaders are encouraged to conduct comprehensive assessments, prioritize investments, and foster a culture of continuous learning and ethical behavior.

For Start-Up Businesses

Start-ups often face unique challenges related to resource constraints and skill gaps. The D^3 Leadership Blueprint provides practical strategies for building a solid foundation, managing resources efficiently, and fostering a positive organizational culture. Start-ups are advised to focus on foundational planning, market research, and leadership development to support growth and resilience.

For Non-Profit Organizations

Non-profits face distinct challenges related to resource limitations and mission-driven objectives. The D^3 Leadership Blueprint offers insights for optimizing resource use, building a skilled team, and maintaining high ethical standards. Non-profit leaders are encouraged to develop effective fundraising strategies, evaluate program effectiveness, and enhance visibility and outreach.

D^3 Leadership Blueprint is Valuable for Established Businesses

Addressing deficits involves a proactive approach to identifying and overcoming gaps. The D^3 Leadership Blueprint offers valuable strategies for established businesses.

- The first step in addressing deficits is conducting a thorough assessment of the organization's current state. This includes evaluating financial performance, assessing team capabilities, and reviewing leadership practices. By pinpointing specific areas of shortfall, leaders can develop targeted strategies to address these issues effectively.

- Effective resource management is essential for addressing deficits. The blueprint advocates for prudent financial, human, and intellectual resource allocation. Leaders should prioritize investments in training, development, and strategic partnerships to fill gaps and enhance organizational capabilities.
- Skills deficiencies can be addressed through targeted training and mentorship programs. The blueprint emphasizes the importance of continuous learning and development, encouraging leaders to invest in professional growth opportunities for themselves and their teams. This approach builds a more competent workforce and fosters a culture of innovation and adaptability.
- Addressing deficits in leadership character requires a commitment to ethical behavior and personal growth. The blueprint draws on biblical principles, such as the parable of the talents (**Matthew 25:14-30**), to highlight the importance of stewardship and accountability. Leaders are encouraged to model ethical behavior, promote a culture of integrity, and continuously reflect on their leadership practices.

D³ Leadership Blueprint is Valuable for Start-Up Businesses

Start-ups often face unique challenges related to resource constraints and skill gaps. The D³ Leadership Blueprint provides practical strategies to address the challenges of startups.

- Start-ups must build a solid foundation from the outset. The blueprint offers guidance on resource allocation, skill development, and character building, helping start-ups establish a solid base for growth and success.
- Start-ups typically operate with limited resources, making efficient management critical. The blueprint advises start-up leaders to prioritize investments in key areas and seek creative solutions to address resource constraints.
- Building a positive organizational culture is essential for start-ups. The blueprint encourages leaders to foster a culture of integrity and continuous learning, laying the groundwork for long-term success and resilience.

D³ Leadership Blueprint is Valuable for Non-Profit Organizations

Non-profits face distinct challenges related to resource limitations and mission-driven objectives. The D³ Leadership Blueprint offers valuable insights for non-profit leaders.

- Non-profits often operate with tight budgets and limited resources. The blueprint provides strategies for optimizing resource use, including prioritizing key initiatives and seeking strategic partnerships to enhance impact.

- Non-profits can benefit from targeted training and development programs. The blueprint emphasizes the importance of building a skilled and motivated team, which is crucial for achieving organizational goals and maximizing impact.
- Non-profits are expected to uphold high ethical standards. The blueprint guides non-profit leaders in cultivating a culture of integrity and transparency, ensuring their organizations operate with the highest ethical commitment.

Vision in Action Business Solutions: Consulting Services for Start-Ups, Established Businesses, and Non-Profits

VIABS is the incubator for the work to get done. It is a consulting firm that empowers established businesses, non-profits, and startups to achieve their goals through tailored strategies and innovative solutions. The firm addresses critical challenges, optimizes operations, and fosters sustainable growth. VIABS offers a comprehensive suite of consulting services to help businesses, non-profits, and startups navigate their unique challenges and achieve their goals. By leveraging their expertise in strategy development, operational efficiency, financial management, and leadership, VIABS empowers organizations to thrive and positively impact their respective fields. For more information, visit our website at getviasolutions.com.

Consulting Services for Start-Ups:

1. VIABS assists start-ups in crafting robust business plans that outline their vision, market opportunity, competitive landscape, and financial projections. We help new ventures define their value proposition, develop a clear business model, and set achievable milestones. This foundational planning is critical for securing funding and guiding the business through its initial stages.
2. Understanding the market is crucial for start-ups. VIABS conducts thorough market research to identify target audiences, analyze market trends, and evaluate competitive positioning. We help start-ups develop go-to-market strategies that effectively address market needs and capitalize on growth opportunities.
3. Start-ups often face challenges in managing finances and securing funding. VIABS guides budgeting, financial forecasting, and cash flow management. We assist in preparing pitch decks and grant proposals to attract investors and secure initial funding.
4. VIABS supports start-ups in setting up their operational infrastructure, including selecting technology solutions, establishing processes, and building efficient workflows. We aim to create a solid operational foundation that supports scalability and growth.
5. Building a strong leadership team is essential for start-ups. VIABS offers leadership coaching and team-building workshops to help founders and early-stage leaders develop the skills to guide the organization effectively and foster a positive company culture.

Consulting Services for Established Businesses:

1. VIABS helps established businesses refine their strategic plans, set actionable goals, and identify key performance indicators (KPIs). We analyze market conditions, competitive landscape, and internal processes to develop strategies that drive growth and competitive advantage.
2. VIABS assesses current operational processes and identifies areas for improvement. We employ process optimization techniques to enhance efficiency, reduce costs, and improve productivity. This may include technology implementation, process reengineering, and supply chain management.
3. The consultancy provides expert financial planning, budgeting, and risk management advice. VIABS helps businesses develop financial models, manage expenses, and optimize resource allocation to ensure financial stability and growth.
4. VIABS offers leadership training and coaching to enhance the skills of executives, managers, and emerging leaders. Our programs are designed to build a cohesive leadership team that drives the business forward.
5. VIABS provides market research and growth strategy development for businesses seeking to expand. We assist in market penetration, product diversification, and geographic expansion to support sustainable growth.

Consulting Services for Non-Profits:

1. VIABS works with non-profits to strengthen organizational structures, improve governance, and enhance operational efficiency. We support the

development of strategic plans that align with the organization's mission and community needs.

2. VIABS helps non-profits develop effective fundraising strategies and enhance financial sustainability. This includes identifying funding sources, creating grant proposals, and implementing donor engagement strategies.
3. VIABS provides services for evaluating program effectiveness and measuring impact. We help non-profits establish metrics for success, conduct evaluations, and use findings to refine programs and demonstrate impact to stakeholders.
4. VIABS offers training and development programs tailored to non-profits. This includes workshops on board governance, volunteer management, and strategic planning to build internal capacity and improve operational effectiveness.
5. VIABS assists non-profits in developing marketing strategies to enhance visibility and outreach. These strategies include branding, social media strategy, and community engagement to attract supporters and raise awareness.

Vision in Action Business Solutions provides a broad spectrum of consulting services tailored to the needs of start-ups, existing businesses, and non-profits. Our expertise in strategic planning, operational efficiency, financial management, and leadership development helps organizations achieve their goals and navigate challenges effectively. VIABS helps clients build a solid foundation for growth and success through a customized approach and industry best practices.

For further information on the consulting services provided by Vision in Action Business Solutions, you can refer to the following resources:

Vision in Action Business Solutions website:
www.getviasolutions.com

D[3] Leadership Blueprint Masterclass registration:
www.d3leadershipmasterclass.com/register

Angela Goodman-Foxworth

Angela "AngieFox" Goodman-Foxworth is a native of Sumter, South Carolina. She is married to Shawn Foxworth, a mother to five adult children and ten bonus children, and grandmother to thirty-eight. Angela is an Independent Business Owner, Mentor, Radio Personality, Podcast Host, Certified Life Coach, Certified Mental Health Coach, and Certified in Christian Leadership. She is also a published author and an ordained Evangelist. Angela proudly serves her community as a 2021 graduate of The Sonship School of the Firstborn and a 2022 recipient of Who's Who in America.

Once severely depressed and suicidal, Angela now devotes her life to empowering others to overcome adversity and walk in their purpose. Since her complete deliverance in 2012, she has authored *From Suicide to God's Side*, chronicling her 17-year journey through depression, suicide attempts, and her ultimate deliverance.

Angela is the visionary and founder of **We Are One the Movement**, an organization dedicated to uniting women from all backgrounds and helping them realize and fulfill their dreams. She is also co-owner of **Empowerment Podcast Network** and **Women Inspirational Radio**, online platforms that enable people worldwide to host talk shows designed to inspire and uplift listeners.

Delivered, set free, and made whole, Angela is called to serve, build, encourage, and help everyone she encounters. Her life motto is simple:

"If I can't help you, I certainly won't hurt you."

Chapter 5: I'm Not Just GLAD (*Good Looking At a Distance*), Anymore

Angela Goodman Foxworth

Have you ever been counted out by your family, your community, or even your church? Has someone you loved:

- Left you with the kids?
- Claimed you wouldn't make it without him?
- Taken everything you had?
- Left you badly beaten physically, emotionally, or mentally?
- Left you feeling broken, busted, and disgusted?

Perhaps you've cried yourself to sleep night after night because your heart was shattered. Maybe you've sat on the sidelines of life wondering, *What's wrong with me? Why doesn't anybody want me? How come I am always disregarded?*

If we're honest, we all struggle with something. But if you are tired of merely existing, tired of hurting, and you are ready to truly live again, then declare with me: **"IT'S RESURRECTION TIME!"**

For the benefit of those who don't believe,
For the benefit of those who said you wouldn't be here today,
For the benefit of those who assumed you were dead,

RISE UP!

Say this out loud:

"I have no more time to waste. I will not allow one more summer to pass me by. I am beautiful and wonderfully made, and I will let my inner beauty and strength prevail in my life."

You were created in God's image and beauty. You possess an inner strength that you must tap into to live your best life **on purpose**.

A Story of Struggle and Resurrection

As a once-severely depressed and broken woman, a mother of five young children, daughter to loving parents, sister and friend to many. I know from experience how overwhelming life can be. When life started "lifing," I gave up on myself. For seventeen long years, I surrendered to negative thoughts and bitter, angry emotions. I hated myself, became depressed, and entertained suicidal thoughts. I didn't realize I was experiencing a mental health breakdown; I just assumed it was the "hand I was dealt." So, I came into agreement with all the bad and the ugly, my mindset became more toxic, and so did the words I spoke. Ultimately, my actions turned deadly. I didn't need others to count me out; **I had already assumed myself to be dead.**

My desperation led me to overdose on sleeping pills in an effort to end the pain. That choice launched me on a tumultuous journey of anger, despair, turmoil, and deep disappointment, eventually leading to my death. One cold day in February 2007, I finally did what I had been trying to do since 1995: I ended my life. My body absorbed the poisons, and I believed it was truly over.

However, the doctor who attended to me said that although I had died in route to the hospital, an angelic stranger found me and simply refused to give up. By the time the ambulance reached the emergency entrance, I had a faint pulse. **I WAS RESURRECTED.**

I was given a second chance at life, yet I didn't know how to live. My mindset hadn't changed; my body had been revived, but my mind was still a mess. The transformation I needed in my mind had not occurred. So, I continued that destructive path, attempting to end my life again and again until 2012, when everything changed. I woke up! I decided to apply the tools I learned in counseling alongside the keys I discovered in God's Word, and I changed. My thinking changed. My speech changed. And my actions changed. I was set free. I finally realized that life was worth living.

Becoming a Better Me

Years later, I am still here; not who I once was, but a better version of myself: a stronger me, a wiser me, a happier me, a healed me. The woman who once believed every negative, ugly thing that plagued her mind is gone. In her place stands a woman who believes what God says about her. She lives as an overcomer, **more than a conqueror**, the head and not the tail, healed, delivered, and whole. That woman is **unstoppable**. That woman is **me**. And that woman is **you**.

It's you, because life doesn't dictate **who** you are or **who** you become. Your true beauty and greatest strength come from within. You are who God created you to be; not your circumstances, not your mistakes, not your failures, nor your disappointments, or even what "they" say about you. You **rock**. So, rise up from the ashes of your past and **LIVE**!

When negative thoughts and ideas try to invade your mind, cast them down and replace them with good, positive ones. When life doesn't turn out quite the way you hoped, shake the dust from your feet and move on. Refuse to set up camp in the land of defeat. You have too much to accomplish to remain stuck. Remember, failure only wins when you stop trying.

I cannot count how many times I've had to start over. For the longest time, I believed I would never find my niche. Even after being resurrected and renewing my mindset, I still didn't know how to live life to the fullest. That's when I decided to use my journey to help others, which required education. I became a Certified Mental Health Coach and eventually a Certified Mental Health Advocate. Armed with these and other certifications, I felt equipped to help those struggling with depression, suicidal thoughts, and other mental health challenges. **Now, I'm finally living my life on purpose, for a purpose.** I'm ready, willing, and able to guide others in obtaining and sustaining mental wellness.

From "G.L.A.D." to Genuine Living

I'm no longer content with just being "GLAD", *Good Looking At a Distance.* That phrase simply describes faking it, appearing as though everything is okay when, in reality, it's not. You might look like you have it all together, but behind that mask lies a broken mess. Living behind masks of shame, guilt, condemnation, self-pity, anger, or untreated mental health issues prevents you from living your best life. The true you, the one God wants, is truly happy, fulfilled, successful, effective, and productive.

I remember pretending to be fine in front of others. It was exhausting. I had to fake smiles, laughter, and even the energy to get up and go. I consistently lied to everyone about my condition and refused to ask for help. When my family, friends, and co-workers found out about my suicidal tendencies, they didn't believe it. They were convinced the doctors had confused me with someone else, until the attempts continued. Yes, I know firsthand the exhaustion of living a lie. It is so much better to live in truth and *be* what you appear to be.

Today, my smile is genuine. My laughter is loud and real. When I say, "I'm good," I mean it. My dancing eyes reflect that joy. No more merely existing, I'm truly **living** and enjoying the journey.

Mindset Matters

I firmly believe that losing is not an option. Once you are determined to live, you **will** live. It starts in your heart and mind, because your mind is a powerful tool. "As a man thinketh, so is he." If you allow your thoughts to be unhealthy, your life will follow suit. Just as you seek medical help for physical illnesses or spiritual help for spiritual weaknesses, it is vital to seek help for mental health issues as well. Failing to do so allows your mind to remain stuck in unchallenged negativity.

To experience a healed mind and achieve mental wellness so that you can do, have, and become all you were created to be; you must actively engage in the process. **Since every action begins as a thought, here are a few ways to help maintain a positive mindset**:

1. **Challenge every negative thought** – Practice positive affirmations.
2. **Cultivate self-compassion** – Treat yourself with kindness and understanding.
3. **Set and reach attainable goals** – Celebrate small victories along the way.
4. **Celebrate yourself unapologetically** – Recognize your achievements and worth.
5. **Utilize available resources** – Consider support groups, family, friends, therapy, and other tools.
6. **Learn from your past** – Embrace the journey of healing and wholeness.

Never allow mistakes or setbacks to keep you bound. Remember, **every setback** is an opportunity to grow, to do better, and to have better. Once you determine in your mind to live totally healed spiritually, socially, physically, and mentally, take the necessary steps to be **empowered**. *Why?* Because when you are empowered, you can empower others. It's not enough to find help and thrive; you must also throw out a lifeline to those around you so they can live too. Your family, the next generation, your community, city, state, nation, and even the world depends on **you**.

Embrace Your Champion Within

One of the greatest gifts we have is life itself. I believe we do God and ourselves a disservice when we fail to live the abundant life He desires. In our ordinary, everyday routines, working, going to school, and taking care of daily responsibilities, we must recognize the champion inside us. It's time to awaken and release that champion. The best time to start **living** is right now, because it doesn't matter how you begin or how you arrive at this point, what truly matters is how you choose to end. Your ending is determined by what you do with the time you have.

Will you sit down and give up? Will you feel sorry for yourself and walk away? Or will you pick yourself up, dust yourself off, and keep fighting? Yes, **fighting,** because life is a fight every single day. But it's a fight you can win. It's a fixed fight, and you cannot lose as long as you trust God, love yourself, and do the work to reach your goals. You will emerge on top of your world.

The first day of the rest of your life begins when you decide not just to be "GLAD" anymore but to **Get Up, Dress Up, and Show Up** for yourself. Show up with love, joy, peace, and a sound mind. Live a life that is **whole, free, and totally healed,** and in doing so, you will offer hope and healing to others.

It's your time. Rise up and live.

Connect with me:

Facebook:
https://www.facebook.com/TheAngieFoxShow

DANIEL J. WILLIAMS

Daniel J. Williams is a leader in the space of men's mindset & performance coaching, a podcast personality, published author, and spirited keynote speaker. The platform he manages is called ACT ACCORDINGLY Men's Mindset & Performance, AAMMP for short. What makes AAMMP unique and successful is its strategies of course correction we utilize to identify and address faulty beliefs and mindset. After all, thoughts happen before actions and activities do.

Daniel believes balance is a harder objective to obtain than harmony. Harmony allows a man to realistically manage himself along with every other responsibility circulating in his life. Balance on the other hand is always weighing one responsibility against the other.

A man possessing spiritual, emotional, mental, and physical harmony is poised to become and remain whole, centered, and progressive. Every man's personal, professional, relational, and financial sphere of stability and longevity hinges on harmony for him to be both effective and impactful.

Daniel himself did an about-face in his own life using the same biblical principles and strategies he offers in his AAMMP community and courses. He has risen from extramarital affairs, divorce, being a presently absent father, alcohol and substance abuse, homelessness, the loss of his self-confidence to being today a man of God, coach, and advocate for men to reassess, recalibrate, and reintroduce themselves.

Daniel J. Williams. ACT ACCORDINGLY
Website: https://2actaccordingly.com/

Chapter 6: Courage to Change, Act Accordingly

Daniel J. Williams

A Williams man doesn't know how to be with just one woman, it's not in their nature. That was the joke about the men in my family. We were reputed to be incapable of limiting ourselves to one woman and remaining faithful, even in marriage.

Proverbs 23:7 (KJV)
"For as he thinketh in his heart, so is he."

I took on that tradition of the Williams man and became a womanizer, too. I believed it was in my DNA. I never saw any man in my family demonstrate true monogamy, so it was easy to adopt that mindset and live by it.

Multiple Girlfriends, Even in Marriage

William's men commonly kept multiple girlfriends, even if they were married. Marriage never stopped them from living like single men, unable to decide whether they wanted to be with *this* woman, *that* woman, or *the other* woman.

James 1:8 (KJV)
"A double minded man is unstable in all his ways."

Unconsciously, the men in my family were showing me how to be undisciplined and gluttonous jumping from woman to woman, unable to make a decision and stick to it. Needless to say, I followed suit, living in a state of indecision, just like them.

The Clash of Old and New

A man isn't meant to live without discipline for a portion of his life and then magically decide to embrace discipline later. When that happens, the irresponsible habits you've cultivated will clash with the responsible habits you're trying to establish. At that intersection, the undisciplined version of you will resist the disciplined version you should have always been and now want to become.

Romans 7:18-19 (GNT)
"[18] For even though the desire to do good is in me, I am not able to do it.
[19] I don't do the good I want to do; instead, I do the evil that I do not want to do."

As I got older, I often experienced these tug-of-war moments. Part of the reason was that my life no longer remained void of examples of men who lived contrary to what I had grown up seeing. Once you discover the difference between an inappropriate choice and an appropriate one, you must confront your own actions.

Recognizing Healthy Examples

I'm not dismissing anyone's childhood trauma or memories. Many of us grew up without seeing healthy relationships, regularly. But in most cases, at some point, even if briefly, we did catch glimpses of healthier dynamics between men and women, husbands and wives, and fathers with their children. It might not have been every day, but it was enough to show us that there was another way. Would you say I'm inaccurate or accurate?

We have commonly used the excuse that we have difficulty being faithful husbands or present fathers because we didn't see that in our own homes. Yet, in my opinion, because we know what it's like to be hurt or disappointed, we at least know what **not** to do. Even if we don't have the entire list of "right" things, we certainly know the "wrong" things to avoid.

Our start was only that: **a start**; not our end.

Ecclesiastes 7:8 (ESV)
"Better is the end of a thing than its beginning..."

Children don't know the difference between right and wrong until someone teaches them. If a child only sees inappropriate behavior, they'll assume it's normal. They can't recognize it as wrong. That's why it's crucial for men to say, *"This is the honorable way to live,"* and then demonstrate it by our actions.

Titus 2:6-7 (GNT)
"[6] In the same way urge the young men to be self-controlled.
[7] In all things you yourself must be an example of good behavior."

No More Hiding Behind Excuses

At this point, we can't hide behind excuses like, *"I never saw a good father or a man who was faithful to one woman."* God never allows us only to experience hardship; He ensures that we see glimpses of hope and possibilities. Midnight lasts an hour, and then the next hour arrives, eventually giving way to sunlight and a new day.

Psalm 30:5 (KJV)

"Weeping may endure for a night, but joy cometh in the morning."

If we're honest, God has allowed us opportunities, maybe not daily or to our preferred extent, to see men of character and integrity. We've seen men being honorable to their wives in certain instances. We've witnessed sincere affection from a father to his children at some point. We've also seen how some men are held in high esteem by others, even in their absence. Though it might not have been our everyday reality, we discovered that men like this do exist, standing in contrast to what we once believed was "normal."

The Pain of Preventable Losses

I believe the greatest losses that can wound a man are those he could have prevented, and those are the losses that we are personally responsible for. Often, it's only after the damage is done and someone is gone for good that we realize how valuable they were to us.

My first wife was a good woman, both *to* me and *for* me, yet I never treated her like one. I remained a "single" man in my mind. On the day we exchanged vows, I still had a girlfriend I was sleeping with. So why did I propose and exchange vows in the first place? Selfishness leads to foolish decisions. Thus, I got married while still behaving like a single man throughout our marriage. I provided for her financially but completely failed to honor my emotional responsibilities.

The same negligence applied to my children. They knew I loved them, but I wasn't there for them as often as I should have been, due to juggling a full-time job, a part-time job, multiple women, and my alcohol and cocaine habits. Essentially, I was a *presently absent* father: physically there but sporadically available emotionally.

A Moment of Clarity

My sobering moment came on a weekend when I decided to stay home and pretend to be a family man. I sat there, listening to my family's stories and experiences, noticing they were all laughing about things I had no clue about. It was like a movie scene where the camera pans out, slows down, and the main character realizes he's a stranger in the middle of his own family.

While Jermaine was off doing his own thing, his family was creating memories without him. (Jermaine is my middle name and what most people called me growing up. I later chose to go by Daniel, my first name, believing it sounded more mature.)

In that moment, I realized they had learned to be a family without me. I didn't know what was worse, feeling like a stranger among those I provided for, not being able to contribute to their shared experience, or the realization that they didn't **need** me to build lasting memories.

Did I do an immediate 180-degree turnaround that day? No. I did better for a little while, but as the saying goes, old habits die hard. Eventually, those old habits won again.

James 4:7 (GNT)
"So then, submit yourselves to God. Resist the Devil, and he will run away from you."

The Downward Spiral

Why didn't I change? Because I chose the path of least resistance. I wanted to change, but the mindset I'd adopted had become a wall I couldn't break through. Brother, let me warn you: don't allow yourself to become a slave to self-destructive habits.

My marriage fell apart. My wife was done with empty apologies and wanted a divorce. My children were tired of my constant disappointments and wanted a reliable father. I lost my family because I chose myself one too many times.

Proverbs 16:25 (NKJV)
"There is a way that seems right to a man, But its end is the way of death."

The divorce happened, and my wife and children left. I spiraled deeper into more women, more alcohol, and more substance abuse until I couldn't recognize myself. It wasn't until I reached the point of feeling total dissatisfaction with who I'd become, that I asked God to sober my thinking and restore my family. By then it was too late to save the marriage; the divorce went through. Thankfully, over time, she forgave me, and we remain friends. My kids gradually grew comfortable with me again, but only after seeing consistent stability, combined with personal conversations to rebuild the trust and confidence I had destroyed.

Lessons Learned: A Warning and Suggestions

I'm sharing my story to spare you from having a similar one. If your marriage is on the brink of collapse but still has a chance:

1. **Apologize with Changed Behavior**
   Let your actions speak louder than any "I'm sorry." Transform into the opposite of the man who created the marital problems.
2. **For Single Men**
   - Refrain from random dating.
   - Invest time in discovering your likes and dislikes.
   - Build spiritual, emotional, relational, and professional stability.
   - Establish a solid, reputable name for yourself in various professional circles.
   - Create a long-term plan so you can genuinely enjoy your future family rather than working around the clock to survive.
   - Become a husband before you become a father.

Proverbs 22:1 (AMP)

"A good name [earned by honorable behavior, godly wisdom, moral courage, and personal integrity] is more desirable than great riches, And favor is better than silver and gold."

Conclusion: Time to Act Accordingly

As a man, I'm concerned about the traps we allow future generations to walk into. As both a man and a men's mindset/performance coach, I am committed to uplifting, encouraging, and guiding my brothers to be men who are respected, admired, valued, and loved. To do that, we must first accept accountability and be willing to endure the pain of the healing process.

We have to acknowledge our faults and strive for genuine transformation. It won't be easy, but **it's worth it because we're worth it**. If you agree, let's go—let's get it done.

Let's ACT ACCORDINGLY.

Connect with me:

Website: https://2actaccordingly.com/

Ericia R. Turner

Ericia R. Turner is a dedicated educator and community leader who resides in Sherrills Ford, North Carolina. With a passion for fostering growth and excellence in public education, Ericia has devoted 25 years to various roles, including teacher, coach, assistant principal, principal, and Director of Athletics. She is currently serving as Executive Director of Athletics for Charlotte Mecklenburg Schools. Her extensive background has allowed her to positively impact the lives of students and athletes throughout her career.

Ericia received both B.S. and M.S. degrees in Physical Education from North Carolina Agricultural and Technical State University. She also obtained a School Administration Certification from Gardner Webb University and holds an Ed.S. Degree in Educational Leadership from the University of North Carolina at Greensboro. Currently, she is enrolled in a Doctoral Program to further enhance her knowledge and expertise in the field of education.

As a proud parent of two children, Ericia balances family life while also being a caregiver to an elderly father, exemplifying a commitment to family values and support. In addition to educational leadership, Ericia has a profound commitment to faith, serving as an Associate Minister at Mt. Zion Baptist Church in Hickory, NC, and was ordained in November 2024. Recently, Ericia embarked on a new venture as the CEO and Founder of Ericia R Turner Executive Coaching and Leadership Development, LLC. Through her business she aims to provide executive coaching and leadership development services to professionals seeking to enhance their skills and reach their full potential.

Throughout her career, Ericia has been recognized for excellence in leadership, receiving accolades such as the Charlotte Mecklenburg Schools Principal of the Year (2020-21), North Carolina Southwest Region Principal of the Year (2021), and North Carolina Athletic Director of the Year (2023). Her dedication to student success and community engagement continues to inspire those around her.

Ericia's ability to overcome challenges and turn adversity into opportunity is evident through her adaptability, determination, strategic collaborations, and commitment to empowering others. Her journey serves as a testament to the transformative power of resilience and the ability to find hidden opportunities within setbacks.

Chapter 7: Unveiling the Unseen: The Invisible Strength of African American Women in Leadership

Ericia R. Turner

You may write me down in history
With your bitter, twisted lies,
You may trod me in the very dirt
But still, like dust, I'll rise.

Does my sassiness upset you?
Why are you beset with gloom?
'Cause I walk like I've got oil wells
Pumping in my living room.

Just like moons and like suns,
With the certainty of tides,
Just like hopes springing high,
Still I'll rise.

— Maya Angelou, "Still I Rise"

In dimly lit corridors of history, a powerful force has woven itself into the fabric of time often hidden, yet undeniably present. African American women have long been the unsung heroes of leadership, defying relentless odds and illuminating the path toward progress. This chapter invites you on a journey to unveil that *invisible strength*, exploring the stories of grace, courage, and unwavering determination that have shaped our collective past.

The Unyielding Power of Rising

Maya Angelou's poem, "Still I Rise," reverberates with the essence of triumph in the face of oppression. Her depiction of rising dust symbolizes an indomitable spirit: once stirred from the ground, that dust forms a cloud and ascends far beyond the forces that tried to keep it down. African American women, too, have risen—again and again—despite racism, sexism, and countless personal challenges.

Did you want to see me broken?
Bowed head and lowered eyes?
Shoulders falling down like teardrops,
Weakened by my soulful cries?

— ***Maya Angelou, "Still I Rise"***

Angelou's words mirror how countless Black women have endured hostility yet continued to stand tall. This resilient spirit is an everlasting testament to their determination and leadership.

Unsung Leaders Through History

When we peel back the layers of history, a rich tapestry emerges—one woven by African American women who devoted themselves to academia, business, civil rights, politics, and more. These achievements confirm that the American Dream is for all, irrespective of race or gender. Women such as:

- **Maya Angelou**: Celebrated poet, author, activist, educator—she leveraged her life stories of struggle and discrimination to influence politics and empower future generations.

- **Madam C. J. Walker**: America's first Black self-made millionaire, pioneering entrepreneurship and philanthropy.
- **Shirley Chisholm**: The first Black woman elected to Congress, challenging political norms and advocating for equity.
- **Rosa Parks**: A Civil Rights icon whose steadfastness helped spark a nationwide movement against segregation.
- **Ida B. Wells, Mary McLeod Bethune, Johnetta Cole, Condoleezza Rice, Mae Jemison**: Exemplars of perseverance, service, and leadership, each forging powerful legacies that guide us today.

Their stories are more than historical footnotes; they are guideposts illuminating the road to inclusive progress. Recognizing these extraordinary women is both a tribute to the past and a call to action for a more equitable present and future.

Embracing Our Legacy and Leading Forward

As an African American woman, I am keenly aware that knowing my past, understanding my present, and moving toward my future is vital. It is a testament to the countless trailblazers who paved the way, often under the weight of oppression. I did not arrive where I am on my own—I stand on the shoulders of legends. By acknowledging and amplifying the voices of African American women in leadership, we construct a more inclusive, prosperous society. We open doors to fresh perspectives, narratives, and innovations.

"For as he thinketh in his heart, so is he."

(Proverbs 23:7, KJV)

This scripture underscores the power of a mindset rooted in confidence and self-worth. I have learned to embrace my greatness and unique qualities, allowing them to shine. My identity is inseparable from my race and gender; they define my heritage and my calling.

Standing Alone at the Table

Have you ever found yourself as the only woman, or the only African American woman, at the table?

This moment is a recurring challenge for many women of color in leadership: navigating boardrooms, executive meetings, and conferences where they are consistently underrepresented. But these moments also reveal tremendous strength and resilience, as our voices bring crucial insights and perspectives.

Owning the Arena

I am currently reading *Own the Arena* by **Katrina Adams**, who became the first African American woman and the youngest President and CEO of the United States Tennis Association. Her words profoundly resonate as she boldly encourages us to embrace our power, break barriers, and conquer obstacles with unwavering resolve. Although being the only woman in the room can feel intimidating, it presents an unparalleled opportunity to shape narratives and inspire others to follow in our footsteps.

Leadership Motivated by Impact

After 25 years in leadership as a teacher, coach, assistant principal, principal, athletic director, executive director, and minister, my motivation is no longer just about personal achievement, it's about making a meaningful impact. As the only Black female District-Level Athletic Director in North Carolina, I recognize the significance of representation for young Black and Brown girls who aspire to careers in athletics. I carry this responsibility seriously, believing that this calling is divinely appointed.

Walking in Your Purpose

Stepping into your purpose requires boldness. Sometimes, we assume that *being chosen* exempts us from *being challenged*. Far from it. In fact, adversity often intensifies when you decide to walk in your purpose. Yet while, embracing your calling means harnessing your strengths, unapologetically. Katrina Adams advocates owning your strengths, weaknesses, and failures. Never let doubt hold you back; be resolutely, fearlessly *you*.

"Expect to Win: Show up as your best self every day."
Carla Harris

Carla Harris's advice resonates: if we expect to win daily, we often do. In her book *Expect to Win*, she speaks of "Carla's Pearls," which remind us that understanding both *who* we are and *whose* we are is essential. When you belong to a higher purpose, nothing can kill what God wants to stay alive.

Finding Support and Moving Your Mountains

Seek out mentors, role models, and allies, people who not only share your vision but also challenge and refine it. You are not alone; countless women have triumphed over similar hurdles, and their experiences remind us that any obstacle can be surmounted.

Remember, *"Elevation Requires Separation."* Not everyone can accompany you on your journey to higher ground. Your alignment could affect your assignment. So, let your conviction speak through your actions and words. Your ideas matter, and your leadership has the power to reshape corporate cultures, educational landscapes, and community environments.

Step Into Your Full Potential

Are you feeling stuck, overwhelmed, or uncertain about your next steps?

As a certified life coach, I stand ready to assist you in identifying limiting beliefs, clarifying your vision, and crafting actionable plans for personal, professional, and spiritual growth. My supportive, empathetic approach is tailored to meet *your* needs, ensuring that each step forward is a strategic and confident one.

It's time to break the proverbial glass ceilings and lead with confidence and strength, just as so many extraordinary women before us have done. You are a trailblazer, a visionary, and a leader who deserves guidance and support.

Together, We Rise!

If you're ready to unlock your full leadership potential, consider partnering with **Ericia R. Turner Executive Coaching and Leadership Development, LLC**. I invite you to take the first step:

1. **Visit our website**: **www.ericiarturner.com**
2. **Schedule your free consultation**: Learn how we can collaborate to propel you to new heights of success.

You are powerful, born to stand out and destined to make a lasting impact. Stand boldly in your uniqueness, remain fearless in your purpose, and remember that, like the dust Maya Angelou described, you, too, will rise.

I rise
I rise
I rise.

— Maya Angelou, "Still I Rise"

Jacqueline Belk-Scott

Jackie Belk-Scott is a wife and mother of 3 who is passionate about lifting and supporting women. She is an author, national speaker, and trainer who leverages her executive leadership experience and skills to tap into the strengths of her clients and build their capacity to excel. Trained in both Law and Business, Jackie is an experienced executive known for strong people, and strategic skills. With over 25 years of multi-sector experience including government, private and non-profit sectors, she provides her clients with practical insights and strategies to help them rise above and beyond to achieve their goals. Jackie has gained a reputation for using creativity and innovation to help her clients make decisions, solve problems, and develop strategies that deliver outcomes with measurable results.

Guided daily by her faith, Jackie adopted **Isaiah 50: 4-7** as her life scripture. Keeping faith and family at the center of all she does, Jackie finds joy in spending time with her crew. Whether gathered as a family watching their favorite sports teams; binging the newest series or movie; or just enjoying a good laugh over a silly joke, she believes it's these simple moments in life that provide her with the most clarity of purpose.

Jackie is a sought-after speaker and consultant across government, non-profit, and private sectors. She also serves as a consultant, lecturer, and trainer for numerous academic, state, local, private, and nonprofit organizations. Jackie has been featured in the book ***How to Be an Emotionally Intelligent Leader*** **by Cheryl O'Donoghue** and is a featured collaborative author in three publications: **Reinvented to Rise II, On Purpose Woman,** ***and Visionary Leaders of Purpose.***

Jackie holds a dual BA from Georgetown University; a Juris Doctor from the Georgetown University Law Center; and a Masters degree in Leadership from the McDonough School of Business at Georgetown. She also studied Pastoral Counseling at Loyola University in Maryland.

As a mentor-coach Jackie's mission is to walk alongside women and support them in their journey to embrace their true selves, leverage their strengths and harness their power.

Chapter 8: Reclaiming Your Voice: The Journey to Overcoming Workplace Trauma

Jacqueline Belk Scott

In the high-stakes world of executive leadership, women often face unique challenges that can undermine their confidence and sense of self-worth. In what should be a space fostering our creativity, collaboration, professional growth, advancement, and fulfillment; the workplace, has increasingly become a battleground for many high performing women. We often find ourselves navigating a complex web of expectations, biases, and challenges, leading us to experience significant stress. When taken together these can cause us undiagnosed trauma that can undermine us at our core. Workplace trauma, whether from overt discrimination, subtle microaggressions, or systemic biases, can deeply impact our ability to lead authentically and effectively. This chapter aims to provide you with tools to identify and process the impact of workplace trauma, reclaim your voice, and emerge as a confident, authentic leader.

Imagine an outwardly successful, high-performing leader who, despite her achievements, constantly questions her worth and feels like an imposter. She navigates an environment where microaggressions are a daily reality and faces systemic biases that challenge her at every turn. She is me. Now, layer on the complexity of race. As a woman of color in leadership, I continuously balance the intersection of race, gender, and expectations. I've experienced being overlooked, underestimated, and subjected to subtle racial biases that eroded my confidence. Unfortunately, my story is not unique. It reflects the broader experiences of many women of color in leadership and many women leaders overall. But let me assure you, while the journey to reclaiming your voice, confidence, and power can be challenging, it is possible and profoundly transformative.

Understanding Workplace Trauma

Workplace trauma encompasses a range of experiences that can have lasting effects on an individual's mental, emotional, and physical well-being. It can include verbal abuse, bullying, discrimination based on race or gender, and harassment among other things. These experiences can be overt, such as being passed over for promotions or subjected to derogatory comments, or more covert, like being excluded from important meetings or decision-making processes. For women of color in leadership, this trauma often also includes microaggressions, and systemic biases.

The mental health impact of workplace trauma can be significant. The psychological and emotional repercussions are far-reaching. Victims often experience symptoms such as anxiety, depression, low self-esteem, and difficulty trusting others. These emotional wounds can significantly impact their ability to function both personally and professionally.

Moreover, the physical manifestations of workplace trauma cannot be ignored. Chronic stress, difficulty sleeping, headaches, loss of appetite, hypertension, and heart disease are some of the most common physical conditions experienced. The compounded effect of these symptoms, along with the toll on your mental and emotional health can severely undermine one's ability to perform and thrive in leadership roles. These effects underscore the importance of addressing this issue holistically.

For women of color, the impact of workplace trauma is often intensified by additional layers of cultural and societal pressures. The expectation to always perform exceptionally well to counteract stereotypes, the need to constantly prove oneself, and the lack of representation in leadership roles (being the *only* or *first*) can all contribute to a heightened sense of isolation and stress. Recognizing and understanding these unique challenges as part of my leadership journey was the first step toward healing and reclaiming my voice.

Recognizing the Signs and Impact

The impact of workplace trauma can sneak up on you, show up in aspects of your life, and manifest in ways you might not immediately recognize. For example, common symptoms of unprocessed trauma include difficulty concentrating, restless or interrupted sleep, persistent sadness, irritability, mood swings, fatigue, muscle tension, and feelings of anxiety when preparing to go to work. These symptoms can significantly impair our ability to lead effectively.

In the workplace, trauma often leads to behaviors like self-doubt, self-sabotage, and imposter syndrome. In my case, self-doubt manifested as me constantly questioning my abilities and decisions. For instance, I frequently second-guessed myself, fearing that any mistake would confirm my alleged unworthiness. Self-sabotage can cause you to engage in behaviors that undermine your success, such as procrastination or setting unrealistic goals. Imposter syndrome is the persistent feeling of being a fraud despite evidence of competence and success. Often, the triggers linked to traumatic workplace experiences cause many high-performing women to feel they do not deserve their accomplishments and live in fear of making mistakes.

Workplace trauma also contributes to the silencing of women leaders. Fear of retaliation, shame, and the desire to protect their careers often prevent women from speaking out about their experiences. This culture of silence can create a toxic environment and allow bad actors to continue their harmful behaviors.

TIP 1: *To help you identify the signs of workplace trauma in your life, here is a self-assessment exercise. Reflect on the following questions:*

1. Do you frequently second-guess your decisions and abilities?
2. Do you set unrealistic goals for yourself and feel devastated when you do not meet them?
3. Do you feel like you must work twice as hard to prove your worth?
4. Do you experience physical symptoms like headaches, muscle tension, or interrupted sleep?
5. Do you feel isolated or unsupported in your workplace?

If you answered "yes" to several of these questions, it is possible that you are experiencing the effects of workplace trauma. Recognizing these signs is the first step towards healing and reclaiming your voice.

TIP 2: *Now, it's time to journal, try answering these questions during your self-reflection time:*

- Reflect on your experiences as a woman leader. Have you encountered any of the challenges mentioned

above? How have these challenges impacted your career? Personal life?
- List instances where you silenced your own voice due to fear or shame. What prevented you from speaking up?
- Reflect on experiences in the workplace that made me feel undervalued. How have these experiences impacted your sense of self-worth.

By identifying and acknowledging your feelings, you are taking a major step towards healing. You can gain greater insight into your emotions and responses and begin to process them more effectively.

The Path to Healing

Acknowledging and validating your experiences is crucial in the healing process. It's important to recognize that your feelings of self-doubt, anxiety, and stress are valid responses to the trauma you've endured. It is essential to listen to your body and mind and seek support when needed. Seeking professional help from a therapist or counselor specializing in trauma can be invaluable. Therapy provides a safe space to process emotions, develop coping mechanisms, and learn healthy ways to manage stress.

Self-care is paramount in the healing process. Prioritizing physical health through exercise, nutrition, and relaxation techniques is crucial. Establishing healthy boundaries is another essential component. This involves learning to say *no*, setting limits on work hours, and protecting your personal time.

Mindfulness and meditation are also powerful tools for you to use. Mindfulness practices help you stay grounded and present, reducing anxiety and stress. Simple meditation exercises, such as focusing on your breath for a few minutes each day, can help you develop a greater sense of calm and control. Additionally, mindfulness helps in recognizing and accepting your emotions without judgment, which is a critical step in the healing process.

Building a strong support system is also vital for healing. Connecting with friends, family, or supportive colleagues can provide you with emotional support and a sense of belonging. Having someone to reach out to, someone I trusted was key. Knowing I was not alone in my journey made all the difference in the world.

Lastly, forgiveness may seem counterintuitive, but it can play a significant role in healing. This may have been one of the toughest parts of my journey. Gaining clarity around the role forgiveness played in my healing was a gamechanger. Forgiveness does not mean you condone the behavior but rather it's the key to releasing the anger and resentment holding you back. It is important to remember that forgiveness is a personal journey, and it may take time.

TIP 3: *Develop a Self-Care Plan…and WORK THE PLAN!*

- Create a personalized self-care plan that includes activities you find relaxing, rejuvenating, and fun. Remember, its ok to laugh, it's the best medicine!
- Identify healthy boundaries you can implement in your personal and professional life. Make a list and post them where you can see them as reminders for accountability.
- Make a list of potential support systems, including friends, family, and professional resources. Keep it nearby where its easily accessible. Schedule times on your calendar to "check-in" or "touch-base". This can be a quick text, email, phone call, or facetime.

The Role of Faith and Spirituality on your Healing Journey

For many women, faith and spirituality provide a profound source of comfort, strength, and guidance during challenging times. I am one of those women. Incorporating aspects of faith and spirituality into my healing process strengthened my sense of purpose, connection to something larger than myself, and hope for the future. Spiritual practices, like prayer, meditation, or connecting with a higher power, can provide comfort, strength, and guidance in the midst of your trauma experience. These practices will be effective to help ground and center you, fostering a deeper connection to your inner wisdom and purpose.

During my journey I found the following very helpful:

- **My search for meaning:** When I was struggling to understand "why" my faith helped me find meaning in my experiences, even amidst suffering. By exploring my beliefs and values, I developed a deeper understanding of my own resilience and inner strength.
- **Connecting with a higher power:** I found comfort in community. By connecting with my higher power and my spiritual community I felt supported, received guidance, and unconditional love. Additionally, by seeking guidance from a spiritual leader I had additional support and encouragement on the healing journey.
- **Engaging in spiritual practices:** Practices such as meditation, prayer, and yoga can promote relaxation, reduce stress, and foster inner peace. These activities helped ground me in the present moment and cultivate a sense of calm…despite the storms swirling around me.

It is important to note that the role of faith and spirituality varies greatly from person to person. Some women may find great comfort in their religious beliefs, while others may prefer a more secular approach to spirituality. Regardless of one's beliefs, incorporating spiritual practices into the healing process can be a powerful tool for personal growth and transformation.

TIP 4: *Try this Spiritual Reflection Exercise when you Journal*

- Reflect on your spiritual beliefs and practices. How have they supported you in the past?
- Explore ways to incorporate spirituality into your healing journey. This could involve attending religious services, spending time in nature, or engaging in meditation or prayer.

Reclaiming your Voice and Building Confidence

Workplace trauma can often lead to a loss of voice. Despite being in a leadership role we are often silenced, intimidated, or made to feel unsure of ourselves. Reclaiming your voice is a crucial step in the healing process and essential for personal and professional growth.

One strategy to conquer self-doubt and self-sabotage involves developing the ability to engage in positive self-talk and self-affirmation. Affirmations are positive statements that reinforce your strengths and capabilities. For example, you might say to yourself, "I am a capable and competent leader," or "I deserve success and recognition." Repeating these affirmations daily can help shift your mindset from one of self-doubt to one of confidence and self-belief.

Visualization techniques are another great strategy for building confidence. Visualization involves imagining yourself in your desired state. By regularly visualizing positive outcomes, you train your brain to focus on success rather than failure. For instance, before an important meeting, you might visualize yourself speaking confidently, making persuasive arguments, and leading with confidence.

We talked about setting boundaries earlier, but they are also relevant here. Boundaries are crucial for protecting your energy and maintaining your mental and emotional health. Learning to say *no* to tasks or responsibilities that are not aligned with your goals or values is an important aspect of boundary setting. While I recognize this is not always possible, particularly if you are leading large bodies of work, if you try hard, I am sure you can find one or two things to say *no* to. Give it a try. For example, if you are constantly asked to take on extra work that undermines your ability to focus on your core responsibilities, it is essential to communicate your limits and prioritize your well-being.

TIP 5: *Try gradually incorporating these practices over the course of your healing journey:*

- **Self-discovery:** Take time to reflect on your values, passions, and strengths. Write them down. Understanding your core identity will help you find your authentic voice.
- **Practice Assertive Communication:** Practice expressing your thoughts and feelings clearly and confidently. Use "I" statements to communicate your needs and boundaries without blaming or accusing others.
- **Building confidence:** Challenge negative self-talk and replace it with positive affirmations. Celebrate your accomplishments, no matter how small.

- **Overcoming fear:** Identify the specific fears that hold you back from speaking up. Write them down. Gradually expose yourself to these fears in a safe and controlled environment to build resilience.

TIP 6: *Try this Voice Journaling Exercise*

- Dedicate a journal to exploring your voice. Write about your thoughts, feelings, and experiences. When were you silenced and how did it feel? When did you use your voice, how did you feel?
- Practice expressing your opinions on different topics, even if you don't share them publicly, write them down.

Conclusion

The journey from *victim* to *victor* is a powerful transformation that is within reach for every woman who has experienced workplace trauma. By understanding the nature of trauma, healing the wounds, and reclaiming your voice, you can embark on a path towards authentic leadership and personal fulfillment.

Remember, healing is a process, not a destination. It is essential to be patient with yourself and celebrate small victories along the way. Surround yourself with supportive people, seek professional help when needed, and prioritize self-care.

As you reclaim your place as a strong, confident, authentic leader, you will have the ability to inspire and empower others. You can influence your workplace by creating a safe and inclusive workplace culture, can break the cycle of trauma, and contribute to a more equitable and just world.

Yes, you!

Your voice matters. Your story matters. Your leadership matters. It is time to reclaim your power and shape your future.

Connect with me via LinkedIn:
https://www.linkedin.com/in/jackiebelkscott/

Marie R. Pringle

Coach Marie R. Pringle, a passionate advocate for mental health and grief support, born and raised in Sumpter, South Carolina. I am a strong, open-minded individual determined to heal and approach life with resilience, passion, and innovative strategies for my clients beyond normal coaching.

When I'm not advocating for mental health, you'll find me on the open road as a dedicated truck driver. Over the past 20 years, I've had the privilege of traversing the country, soaking in its beauty and diversity. Prior to my career in trucking, I worked in a factory where I toiled tirelessly before finding my current path to financial freedom.

Life took unexpected turns during my journey. While my aspirations once led me to dream of a career in law while attending John Jay High School, the loss of my beloved mother to breast cancer at the tender age of 16 reshaped my trajectory. Determined to persevere, I pressed on, fueled by a desire to create a better future for myself and my beautiful family.

However, grief would knock on my door once more. At 29, I bid farewell to my father, succumbing to heart failure. Yet, it was the devastating loss of my daughter to suicide at 48 that brought me to my knees. Grief consumed me, leaving me feeling lost and alone. It was a pivotal moment, a crossroads where I had to confront the depths of my pain and then I learned how to navigate the turbulent waters of grief.

In my darkest hour, I discovered the transformative power of vulnerability and self-compassion. No longer bound by the need to be strong for others, I embarked on a healing journey, to shed the facade of invincibility and embracing humanity.

Driven by a newfound purpose, I turned my pain into a platform for advocacy. Partnering with esteemed individuals like The Street Poet and participating in events like Powerful on Purpose Summit, I amplify the importance of mental health awareness, particularly within the Black community.

As an Eastern Star, unity is ingrained in my essence. I possess qualities of empathy, resilience, and self-awareness, are just a few of the attributes honed through years of advocating for grieving parents and mental health education.

In my quest to empower others, I've gleaned wisdom from esteemed mentors like Dr. Tabatha Russell and Dr. Jewel Rembert. I believe in the urgency of equipping our youth with the tools to navigate life's challenges authentically and embrace their emotions without the fear of shame or blame.

As a life coach, I stand ready to guide you on your journey towards healing and self-discovery. Whether through one-on-one sessions or engaging on social media platforms, I am committed to supporting you every step of the way.

Remember, you are not alone in your struggles. Remove the emblem from your chest and shed the cape from your shoulders. As human beings, we are entitled to experience a range of emotions, we are not characters in a fictional story. In life, stumbling is inevitable, but the key lies in learning how to rise again. Both strength and vulnerability are essential components in the process of growth and healing. Reach out, embrace your truth, and embark on a journey of self-acceptance and growth. Together, we can navigate the complexities of life and emerge stronger, wiser, and more resilient than ever before.

Website: **https://www.breakthroughcoachmarie.com/**

Chapter 9: Echoes of Hope

Marie R. Pringle

The truck's engine thundered through the misty loading dock in McBee, South Carolina. I barely noticed the fog curling around my windows; my mind was absorbed in the rhythmic hum of the vehicle. Each mile I drove took me further from the heavy thoughts that haunted me. Suddenly, a sharp buzz from my phone sliced through my distraction.

On the other end was a friend from my daughter's Nana past. "I want you to hear it from me before you see it on social media," the friend said. A chill rushed over me. I tried calling Nana's number, once, twice, five times, each time met by voicemail. Dread pulsed through me.

My heart was pounding as I phoned my husband, Eric. He was calm, but his voice held an unmistakable note of urgency. "Eric, check the ring camera," I pleaded, voice shaking. I imagined him opening the security app, fear gripping him with every passing second.

Eric's voice faltered when he relayed what he saw: the car was abandoned in the backyard, its brake lights dimming. The house stood in eerie darkness. I gripped the steering wheel tighter, as my knuckles were turning white, and dialed the non-emergency number. I could hardly speak, my hands trembling as I explained the dire situation unfolding at home.

A Nightmare Unfolds

When I finally arrived home, everything beyond my truck's windshield seemed like a surreal haze. I didn't care that I parked haphazardly in the middle of the street and stumbled from the driver's seat; my legs leaden as if weighed down by impending doom.

Police officers moved with grim efficiency around the fogged windows of the car. Their flashing lights illuminated the unsettling stillness inside. Nana was slumped behind the steering wheel, motionless. Every footstep I took felt like an agonizing journey through quicksand, the flashing lights casting haunting shadows against the silent scene.

Moments later, Nana's grandmother arrived, her face etched in confusion and heartache. A coroner followed, and an official's voice rang out: "Who's the mother?" Those words were a jarring jolt of reality. My denial was shattered, as I had desperately hoped they were heading to a hospital, not facing a tragedy's finality. A wrenching scream tore from my soul, shaking my entire being.

The Days After

In the disorienting blur that followed Nana's death, I felt trapped in a nightmare from which I couldn't wake. Planning the funeral was surreal, as if I were moving through someone else's life, selecting a casket, choosing flowers, and picking out clothes. The funeral took place on Sunday, October 10th, at noon. Afterward, well-wishers' calls dwindled. I was left with an overwhelming sense of isolation as if I carried an invisible disease that drove people away.

Family and friends, once pillars of support, felt distant. Their sympathy rang hollow, unable to alleviate my all-consuming grief. The official ruling of Nana's death as a suicide only deepened the torment. This finality widened the gap between me and my loved ones, leaving me questioning what I once believed about love, support, and connection.

Isolation and Introspection

In the weeks after the funeral, I found myself increasingly alone. Family and friends receded into their own worlds of discomfort and helplessness, a stark withdrawal that left me feeling abandoned. This sense of isolation forced me into intense introspection. I clung to anyone who offered even a sliver of kindness, forging fleeting connections with new acquaintances across the country. Extreme couponing became a temporary escape, but each new bond eventually dissolved, leaving me more entrenched in sorrow.

By November 2021, I recognized that I could not move forward alone. I began seeing a therapist, physically present but emotionally distant as I confronted my grief. Guilt and "what ifs" tormented me: *What if I had been home? Could I have been a better mother? Could I have prevented this?* Anger festered inside, sometimes directed at Nana, a bitter truth I struggled to face.

Grappling With Mental Health

My battle with depression and anxiety had started long before I fully understood those terms. Childhood traumas clouded my worldview, leaving me confused and defensive when professionals first mentioned my diagnosis. In my confusion, I turned to social media, oscillating between sharing raw, tearful snapshots of my pain and striving to encourage others despite my own despair.

Memories of Nana ebbed and flowed, each one a poignant reminder of my precious daughter, I had lost. I recall Nana coming out at fifteen and how I immediately embraced her, saying, "I don't care if you like girls or boys. I love all of you. Don't ever think I'll stop loving you because you like girls." I remember Nana's hard-working nature, her love for sneakers, and the radiant smile that brightened any room. Losing such a vibrant soul was a profound shock that underscored the heartbreak of her passing.

A Spiritual Reckoning

Desperate for solace, I sought to strengthen my relationship with God. The therapist, Jewel Renbert, and family friend Michelle Gadson, who had helped with the funeral, became my anchors. Allie, whom I met through a couponing group, would also become another one of my anchors through it all. They regularly checked in, as did influencers like The Street Poet, who offered solace through her platform. Yet, I realized that I had been running from the pain instead of facing it. Confronting the fractures in my relationships and my inner self became unavoidable.

In therapy, I fully acknowledged my lack of emotional intelligence and faced the stark realities of grief. I learned that grief could manifest as debilitating anxiety, explosive anger, or a crushing sense of isolation. Discussions surrounding suicide, especially the pain of losing a child, unveiled an emotional depth I could scarcely comprehend.

Journaling and balloon releases on Nana's birthday and the anniversary of her death became rituals of remembrance.

These moments of reflection highlighted her loss but also served as tentative steps toward healing. I have since poured myself into community events, determined to learn about mental health and the LGBTQ community. Sometimes, it felt like I was merely trying to fill the vast emptiness left by Nana's death, but each endeavor carried the seeds of growth.

Finding a New Purpose

In August 2022, I made a bold decision to go live on social media, this occasion was filled with both excitement and trepidation. The responses I received were immediate and overwhelming. Thousands of followers tuned in, their messages came pouring in, with them sharing their pain, hope, and collective healing. Partnering with The Street Poet, I discovered that my story resonated deeply. I found myself at a crossroads where therapy and the outpouring of empathy guided me toward an unexpected calling, life coaching.

Fueled by the realization that my story could help others, I pursued a Life Coach certification in North Carolina. The live event had not only amplified my social media influence but also shaped a meaningful new career direction I had never anticipated.

A Tale of Loss and Transformation

My story is, at its core, a moving account of grief and renewal. It begins with the shadow of loss, first my parents, then Nana, each death casting an ever-deepening shadow over my life. At first, I stumbled in the wake of these tragedies, seeking any distraction to numb the pain.

However, amid the fog of mourning, the seeds of a deeper purpose took root. Therapy became my battlefield and sanctuary. Each session wove together a fragile sense of hope, piece by piece. Over time, I refused to let Nana's death fade into silence. Instead, I vowed to honor my daughter's memory worldwide, inspiring others who faced similar struggles.

The transition from paralyzing grief to relentless advocacy did not happen overnight. Still, through unwavering determination, I transformed my heartbreak into a powerful instrument of change. I vowed to guide others through the maze of mental health challenges and bereavement. Nana's spirit shone through every word I say, every life I touch, and every endeavor I embark upon.

A Beacon of Hope

Rather than being consumed by my daughter's tragic suicide, I channel my sorrow into a purposeful mission. This mission radiates with hope, borne from my darkest moments. My advocacy stands as a testament to the healing power of transforming anguish into a beacon for others.

In dedicating my life to honoring Nana's memory, I will forever ensure that my daughter's story lives on. Empowered by all who need solace, courage, or validation of their own pain. It is an enduring legacy, a shining reminder of the extraordinary strength within the human spirit when love and determination guide the way. Don't just suffer in silence, seek help and support.

If you would like to schedule a consultation contact:

Website: https://www.breakthroughcoachmarie.com/

Dr. Marquette L. Walker

Dr. Marquette L. Walker is a multifaceted force of inspiration and empowerment, seamlessly blending her roles as a wife, mother, minister, entrepreneur, and author. With a deep commitment to uplifting others, she serves as the founder and owner of Marquette L. Walker Ministries, where she provides spiritual guidance and support to her community. As a devoted wife and mother, Marquette instills the values of faith and resilience in her family, believing that strong relationships are the cornerstone of a fulfilling life.

An acclaimed inspirational speaker, Marquette captivates audiences with her engaging storytelling and heartfelt messages. She is the coach of "Winning Women," a transformative program designed to encourage women from all walks of life to embrace their strength and pursue their dreams. Through workshops and seminars, she empowers her clients to break through barriers and cultivate their unique voices in the world.

Marquette is also the proud author of "Divorced but Not Defeated," a compelling memoir that chronicles her journey of overcoming adversity and finding purpose after personal challenges. Her story resonates with many, serving as a beacon of hope for those navigating similar experiences.

In recognition of her significant contributions to her community and her unwavering dedication to personal growth, Marquette has been awarded an honorary doctorate along with the Presidential Lifetime Achievement Award. These honors reflect her commitment to service and leadership, further solidifying her role as a respected figure in her field.

As the founder of Marquette's Closet and Marquette L. Walker Interior Design, she combines her entrepreneurial spirit with her passion for aesthetics, creating spaces that inspire and reflect the individuality of her clients. Additionally, Marquette co-founded A&M FaithFusion Partners, where she collaborates with like-minded individuals to foster community initiatives and programs.

With a powerful blend of faith, creativity, and compassion, Dr. Marquette L. Walker continues to uplift and inspire those around her, embodying the spirit of resilience and empowerment.

Chapter 10: From Turmoil to Triumph

Marquette L. Walker

My name is **Dr. Marquette L. Walker**, and my life has been a winding path filled with challenges, triumphs, and transformations. Much like the woman at the well in the Gospel of John, I have gone through multiple marriages, each bringing its own share of trials and setbacks. Yet through it all, I have emerged stronger, wiser, and more determined than ever to make a difference in this world.

Growing up, I dreamed of a fairy-tale romance, a perfect marriage, and a happily-ever-after ending. However, life rarely follows the script we imagine. I found myself divorced multiple times, each breakup leaving a scar on my heart and raising many questions about my future.

Rather than succumbing to self-pity or giving up on love entirely, I chose to stand firm and discover strength within my struggles. I leaned on my faith for guidance, taking inspiration from the woman at the well, whose encounter with Jesus transformed her life and gave her renewed purpose.

With a fresh sense of calling, I ventured into ministry. I longed to use my experiences to bring hope and encouragement to others facing similar challenges. Thus, **Marquette L. Walker Ministries** was born: a place where broken hearts could find healing and lost souls could find redemption.

From there, I felt compelled to broaden my outreach to help even more women needing support and direction. This desire led me to establish **Winning Women**, a coaching program designed to empower women to surpass their circumstances and reach their fullest potential. Through one-on-one sessions, group workshops, and motivational speaking engagements, I've motivated countless women to persist in their dreams, no matter how many obstacles stand in their way.

In addition to my ministry and coaching work, I shared my story with the world by writing ***Divorced but Not Defeated***, a candid account of my journey through multiple marriages and the lessons I learned along the way. Through this book, I have connected with readers from diverse backgrounds, offering them reassurance and inspiration in their own battles.

My journey also includes building success in business. I own and operate two thriving ventures: **Destined 4 Greatness II**, an event-planning company, and **Marquette's Closet**. These enterprises allow me to impact my community positively and beyond, using my platform to promote positivity, resilience, and empowerment.

When I reflect on my path, from turmoil to triumph, I am reminded of the extraordinary power of transformation and the unwavering resilience of the human spirit. Every challenge I've faced has made me stronger, more determined, and deeply committed to creating a meaningful impact on the world. I firmly believe that anything is possible with faith, perseverance, and a clear sense of purpose.

Connect with me:

Website: marquettelwalkerministries.com
Facebook: Marquette L Walker and Marquette L Walker Ministries

Sharon Armstrong

Sharon Armstrong is a dynamic and multi-talented individual making waves in the wellness and personal finance industries. As a skilled massage therapist, bodyworker, and coach, Sharon blends the practice of Western and Eastern body manipulation with mindfulness and heart to offer a truly unique and transformative experience for her clients.

Sharon is the visionary behind Azure Touch Body-Mind Connection Centre in Deerfield, Illinois, where she is revolutionizing the way people understand and connect with their bodies. She has developed a series called "Storytelling the Body – How to Read your Body's Messages for Optimal Health and Flow," which is an enjoyable way to learn how to integrate and embody the five elements of Fire, Earth, Metal, Water, and Wood daily.

In addition to her work as a massage therapist, Sharon is also a passionate teacher for young adults and single parents in the area of financial education. As a single mother herself,

Sharon understands the importance of financial literacy and the impact it can have on one's future. She addresses stories of the body as well as financial education in her Azure Health and Wealth speaking platform to engage in healthy conversations for the progress of the world.

"One person can make a difference in people's lives and be a king or queen unto themselves, but one person with a dream of joining with others together can build a kingdom for generations to come," she insightfully shared. Through her speaking engagements and workshops, she empowers others to take control of their health and finances and to live their best lives. Her unique wellness and personal finance approach has helped countless individuals transform their lives and achieve their goals.

Chapter 11: Unlock Your Financial Freedom: The Power of Insurance and Smart Money Management

Sharon Armstrong

Imagine a life where financial constraints don't strangle your dreams. Picture a world where taking a break from higher education isn't a desperate move but a deliberate choice to explore new growth paths. Envision your startup business taking off without the fear of funding shortfalls. Imagine tackling medical bills or long-term care expenses without the looming threat of bankruptcy.

Many of us have found ourselves at a crossroads, needing to pivot due to financial pressures. But is the pursuit of money inherently negative? Absolutely not! The desire for more money often stems from legitimate needs: a health crisis, children's education, relocation, marriage, or the passing of a loved one.

When life's unexpected turns derail your plans, do you throw in the towel or pivot onto a less-traveled path, hoping to reach your destination later? Hold onto your dreams and keep your eyes open; you never know when you'll get back on track.

What if we were taught from the start that pivoting is a natural part of adult life? That we are the generators of our desires, and when circumstances prevent us from generating, we pivot to make our desires happen. This mindset shift could revolutionize how we approach life's challenges.

Let me share a personal story. At 19, I was attending college in New York, with one year left in my pre-med studies. Financially, things got tight. The Pell Grant and Federal Student Loan funds were exhausted, and my parents had relocated from New York to Chicago. Despite my mom's pleas for me to transfer, I felt compelled to finish at my New York college. However, with no funds for my final year, I pivoted, moved to Chicago, and switched my major to Computer Science, the fastest-growing field at the time. I believed this would provide the much-needed financial stability to eventually return to my medical studies.

This wasn't an entirely unexpected situation. I had worked odd jobs to save money, but it wasn't enough. I silently vowed never to be in a position where I didn't control my financial destiny. From then on, I realized that whatever I wanted, whether higher education, a car, or a home, required more money. I needed to increase my income potential to achieve my desired standard of living.

My story is not unique. Even today, "51% of college dropouts cite financial reasons for leaving." Is this preventable? Can parents fully prepare for their children's education? Can you prepare for unexpected medical expenses? Can you prepare for loss of income if the main provider becomes ill or passes away?

Consider the things you value: your home, car, even your cell phone. You insure them because they're valuable to you. Where does the money come from to purchase these items? Was it a gift? Did you earn it through labor or savings? Regardless, the ability to generate income starts with you.

The value begins with you. So, why not insure yourself, the income generator?

The insurance industry dates back to 4000 BCE, when Babylonian merchants used bottomry—loans with the condition that they didn't need to be repaid if the shipment was lost at sea. Most early insurance was for business ventures. The first known life insurance policy was issued on June 18, 1583, in London, where Richard Martin insured William Gybbons for 400 pounds, paying 13 merchants 30 pounds each if Gybbons died within a year. Back then, life insurance primarily ensured a decent burial.

Today, insurance has evolved significantly. Life expectancy has increased, and policies now cover a range of services, including death benefits and living benefits, allowing you to use some premiums for extenuating health circumstances. Life insurance can even serve as a financial tool for retirement and education funding.

The insurance industry has proven its value over a millennium by helping people meet financial challenges. Doesn't it make sense to learn about these programs and get on board?

Because of my life's journey, pivoting due to educational expenses, loss of income from life-threatening accidents, and thriving as an entrepreneur, I can help you. I've successfully helped numerous clients understand money, prepare for life's financial pivots, and reduce financial strain. As a single mother, I've experienced raising a child with student loan debt and two others who are debt-free.

I founded Azure Health and Wealth Investments to teach and coach you on the basics of money: earning, saving, spending, and investing. I prepare you for life's necessities, such as housing, education, and retirement.

At Azure Health and Wealth Investments, I dream of a financially literate world where the toughest decision is about where to go next, not whether or not you can afford to go. A world where you thrive, not just survive. I can teach our young ones to secure their futures using a proven system.

The Power of Financial Literacy

Financial literacy is not just about understanding how to balance a checkbook or manage a budget. It's about making informed decisions that can significantly impact your future. According to a 2019 study by the FINRA Investor Education Foundation, only 34% of respondents could answer at least four out of five financial literacy questions correctly. This statistic highlights a significant gap in our education system.

Imagine if we could close this gap. Imagine a world where everyone understands the basics of investing, saving, and planning for the future. The potential benefits are enormous: reduced debt levels, increased savings rates, and a more financially secure population.

Why Insurance is a Cornerstone of Financial Planning

Insurance is often viewed as an unnecessary expense, but it's a crucial part of any comprehensive financial plan. According to the Insurance Information Institute, in 2020, 54% of Americans had life insurance coverage. However, many are underinsured, meaning they don’t have enough coverage to replace their income for a significant period.

Life insurance isn't just about providing for your loved ones after you're gone. Modern policies offer a range of benefits, from covering medical expenses during critical illnesses to serving as a financial tool for retirement planning. For instance, some policies allow you to build cash value over time, which can be borrowed against for significant expenses like education or home purchases.

Let's Talk Numbers

- **Emergency Savings:** According to a survey by Bankrate, nearly 28% of Americans have no emergency savings. This lack of a financial safety net can lead to high-interest debt and financial instability.
- **Retirement Readiness:** The National Institute on Retirement Security reports that 66% of Millennials have nothing saved for retirement. Proper planning and investment strategies can help ensure a comfortable retirement.
- **Debt Statistics:** The average American household carries $137,063 in debt, according to the Federal Reserve. Understanding how to manage and reduce debt is a critical component of financial health.

Building a Financial Safety Net

In Debt and Financially Overwhelmed: Seek out a pro bono coach who can help you with the fundamentals of personal finance. Attend personal finance classes at a Community College, etc. and have a champion who will encourage you to rise to your next level.

Creating a financial safety net involves several key steps:

1. **Emergency Fund:** Aim to save six months to a year's worth of living expenses. This fund can help cover unexpected costs, such as medical bills or car repairs, without derailing your financial plans. Whenever you use these monies, do replace it to cover future emergencies.
2. **Life Insurance:** Ensure you have adequate life insurance coverage to protect your family. *Consider policies that offer additional benefits, such as critical illness coverage or the ability to build cash value.* You'll never regret this decision.
3. **Disability Insurance:** This type of insurance can replace a portion of your income if you're unable to work due to illness or injury. According to the Social Security Administration, one in four 20-year-olds will become disabled before reaching retirement age.
4. **Retirement Savings:** Start saving for retirement as early as possible. Take advantage of employer-sponsored plans, such as 401(k)s, and consider individual retirement accounts (IRAs) to maximize your savings.
5. **Financial Caregiving** doesn't have a formal definition; it's a term used for family communication. It's telling someone where and with whom your vital papers are kept. As with an attorney, the priest in a plastic bag taped neatly camouflaged in the freezer…wherever the instructions are, someone should know

Educating the Next Generation

One of the most impactful things we can do is educate the next generation about financial literacy. According to a study by T. Rowe Price, only 23% of kids learn about money management in school. Parents play a critical role in filling this gap.

Start by teaching children the basics of budgeting, saving, and investing. Use real-life examples to show them how money works and the importance of making informed financial decisions. Encouraging a healthy relationship with money from a young age can set them up for lifelong financial success. Most Baby Boomers' and older, grew up during a time when financial literacy was neither a part of school curriculum or, spoken about in the home. Let's make this shift for the empowerment of our future generation.

The Role of Technology in Financial Planning

Technology has revolutionized the way we manage our finances. From budgeting apps to online investment platforms, there are numerous tools available to help you stay on track.

- **Budgeting Apps:** Apps like Mint and YNAB (You Need a Budget) can help you track your spending, set financial goals, and manage your budget. Managing your budget is about you telling your money how to work for you, and not you wondering where your money went.
- **Investment Platforms:** Online platforms like Betterment and Wealthfront offer automated investment management, making it easier to grow your savings.
- **Financial Education:** Websites like Khan Academy and Coursera offer free courses on financial literacy, covering topics from basic budgeting to advanced investing.
-

The Importance of Professional Guidance

While technology offers valuable tools, there's no substitute for professional financial advice. A financial advisor can help you create a personalized financial plan, taking into account your unique circumstances and goals.

According to a study by Vanguard, working with a financial advisor can add about 3% in net returns to your portfolio annually. This increase comes from various factors, including portfolio management, behavioral coaching, and financial planning.

A Personal Touch

Let me share another personal story. A few decades ago, I experienced a significant financial setback due to a car accident that almost left me paralyzed. The medical bills piled up, I had a 4-year-old to care for, and I was unable to work for almost a year. Thankfully, I had both health and disability insurance, which covered my medical expenses and provided a portion of my income during my recovery. This experience reinforced the importance of having a robust financial safety net.

As I navigated this challenging time, I realized that many people didn't have the same safety net or access to the strategies that allowed them to build and sustain wealth that resonated with their lifestyle and values. This realization inspired me to help others to build their financial resilience. At Azure Health and Wealth Investments, I focus on providing personalized financial education and coaching to help you prepare for life's unexpected events. What makes us unique is our ability to empower individuals to discover and harness the rhythms of nature that ensure sustainability and lead with a lifestyle of health - building wealth from the inside out.

Fun Facts and Stats to Lighten the Mood:

1. **Did You Know?** The average American spends $1,200 a year on fast food. Imagine investing that in a retirement fund instead!
2. **Life Expectancy Leap:** In the early 1900s, the average life expectancy was around 50 years. Today, it's over 77. That's 27 more years to enjoy life—if you're financially prepared.
3. **Student Loan Struggles:** Nearly 70% of college graduates have student loan debt, averaging $30,000 per borrower. But here's a bright spot: those who plan and save can significantly reduce this burden.
4. **Insurance for Pets?** About 2.5 million pets in North America are insured. If we can insure Fluffy, surely we can insure ourselves!
5. **Why Humor Helps:**
   Humor can be a powerful tool in discussing serious topics like finance. It helps to break down barriers, making the conversation more engaging and less intimidating. Plus, who doesn't enjoy a good laugh while learning about important life skills?

Conclusion

Financial literacy and smart money management are keys to unlocking a life of freedom and security. By understanding and utilizing insurance, you can protect yourself, your family, and your future from unexpected financial challenges. At Azure Health and Wealth Investments, we're here to guide you every step of the way. Let's embark on this journey together, ensuring that you not only survive, but thrive in every aspect of your life.

Contact: **Sharon Armstrong**, www.azuretouch.com for a **Free** 45-minute consultation.

ALGRISH C. WILLIAMS, SR.

Renowned Keynote Speaker | Best-Selling Author | Transformative Leader

Algrish C. Williams, Sr. is a decorated U.S. Army veteran, corporate innovator, and influential entrepreneur whose journey embodies resilience and excellence. From humble beginnings in Jamaica to earning accolades like the **Bronze Star Medal** and **Legion of Merit** during his 26-year military career, Algrish's leadership has inspired transformation on every front.

As the **Founder and President of Williams Leadership Consulting** and a **best-selling author**, Algrish empowers leaders to excel through impactful coaching and strategies. His acclaimed books, **"Navigating the Transition"** and **"Lead with Purpose,"** have inspired veterans and professionals worldwide.

A devoted family man and community advocate, Algrish serves on advisory boards, mentors emerging leaders, and fosters inclusive cultures. With advanced degrees and a relentless commitment to service, Algrish C. Williams, Sr. continues to uplift individuals and organizations, leaving an enduring legacy of leadership and impact.

Chapter 12: From Humble Beginnings to Global Leadership: A Journey of Purpose and Resilience

Algrish C. Williams, Sr

The sun was dipping behind the lush hills of the Jamaican countryside, casting long shadows over our tiny hut. Inside, my mother cowered beneath my stepfather's brute force, his anger rising and his fists falling. As a young boy, I sat outside, powerless and confused, wondering how a person could harbor such cruelty. I often prayed for his demise, desperate for relief from the endless nights of terror.

When my stepfather traveled to Canada or the United States for seasonal work, a fragile calm settled over our home. My siblings and I would run barefoot through the countryside, temporarily freed from the poverty that clung to us like a shadow. Despite these fleeting moments of peace, the hardships were ever-present. Food was scarce, comforts nearly nonexistent, and the future felt distant and uncertain. I had heard stories of my father living in America, a place I believed was overflowing with abundance and free from fear. I would soon learn how mistaken I was.

The Foundation of Leadership
Lessons from My Roots in Jamaica

Growing up in Jamaica, hardship was the constant backdrop of my life. Poverty and hunger accompanied me daily, though I didn't fully understand just how poor we were until I left the island. Despite our meager circumstances, my grandparents provided something far more valuable than money. They instilled in me a deep sense of self-worth and believed in me even when I couldn't believe in myself.

From those early experiences, I discovered the core of leadership: the power of community and the value of unwavering support. My grandparents were my first leaders. They taught me that leadership is not about commanding authority but about caring for others and putting people first. They showed compassion, respect, and the importance of education, values that would form the bedrock of my character.

Even in the face of incredible challenges, I learned that adversity can spark true leadership. It's not about having all the answers but being present when it matters mostly for your family, friends, or anyone in need. These lessons from my Jamaican upbringing stayed with me, shaping the person I became and guiding my actions as a soldier, a corporate leader, and eventually, a mentor to others.

We didn't have much. I often wore hand-me-down clothes and walked barefoot, but my grandparents made sure I grasped the significance of hard work, education, and self-respect. My grandmother, especially, helped me see beyond our day-to-day struggles. She urged me to think about the possibilities ahead, not just the difficulties of the moment. In their own way, my grandparents invested in people with time, love, and wisdom. Their example became my first real lesson in leadership: it's about people, not power.

Adversity as a Catalyst Overcoming Early Challenges

When I moved to the United States, I expected a sudden transformation in my life, but new hurdles awaited me. The streets of Boston were not the golden avenues I had envisioned. My Jamaican accent set me apart, and I was mocked for the way I spoke, my skin tone, and my thrift-store clothes. I had left behind the abuse of my Jamaican home only to encounter a different kind of hardship, discrimination, and alienation.

Those experiences hurt deeply, but they also ignited a fire in me. I knew I had something special to offer, even if the world around me failed to see it. My frustration and sadness pushed me toward personal growth and resilience. Navigating a new culture as an immigrant wasn't simple. I often felt lost, uncertain of my place, particularly as a Black boy in America. Still, I found refuge in sports, especially track, where I ran faster than my doubts and insecurities.

Joining the Junior Reserve Officer Training Corps (JROTC) introduced me to leadership. Wearing that uniform was more than a status symbol; it represented responsibility. I wanted to prove I belonged and to ensure that no one else felt the rejection I had experienced. My time in JROTC taught me that leadership extends beyond seeking acceptance; it's about elevating others, as my grandparents once did for me. Adversity, I realized, shouldn't be events that you just survive, it should be used as fuel for growth, empathy, and guiding others to find their voices.

Forging Resilience in the U.S. Army Leadership Under Fire

Joining the U.S. Army immersed me in a new realm of discipline, responsibility, and leadership. My path was far from smooth. Early on, a superior branded me "arrogant" and claimed I would never succeed. His words stung, echoing the painful taunts I had heard in my childhood. Instead of letting them defeat me, I transformed those criticisms into motivation to excel. I discovered that genuine leadership isn't rooted in chasing titles, but in being the kind of person others want to follow.

As a young soldier, I expected my leaders to embody integrity and purpose. When they fell short, I spoke up. This earned me a label of being "difficult," but in retrospect, I recognize that I was merely holding myself and others to a higher standard. This pivotal time forced me to refine my leadership style, centering it on accountability, integrity, and resilience.

Looking back, my hardships proved both a burden and a blessing. The boy who was once mocked and dismissed grew into a man with a clear mission. Every challenge strengthened my resilience, a mental muscle that becomes more robust with each obstacle. In mentoring others, whether in the Army or in corporate spaces, I've seen that people crave recognition and belonging. My focus is on ensuring that no one under my guidance feels marginalized or overlooked. Leadership, at its heart, is about unlocking each person's potential, even when the world tries to silence them.

Leadership Lessons from Failure
Watching and Learning What Not to Do

Throughout my career, I worked under a variety of leaders, some remarkable, others who misused their authority to create toxic workplaces. From these negative examples, I gleaned invaluable lessons on what leadership should never be. Witnessing how power can be wielded selfishly taught me to always prioritize people over personal gain.

My greatest growth as a leader emerged not only from my successes but also from watching failures. In 10 out of the 17 organizations where I served, leaders genuinely cared about their people. They admitted mistakes, showed vulnerability, and treated missteps as opportunities for collective learning. Conversely, I also met leaders who viewed their titles as a license for privilege, disregarding the well-being of their teams. Those observations solidified my belief that real leadership revolves around creating an environment where people can flourish, not a hierarchy where they must endure neglect.

The Role of Mentors
How Accountability Drives Growth

Mentorship has been a cornerstone of my development. From military leaders to high-level advisors, I've been blessed with mentors who believed in my potential, propelled me beyond my comfort zone, and demanded accountability. Their guidance showed me that leadership is less about personal milestones and more about elevating those who follow you.

True mentorship involves more than just advice. It requires fostering an environment where people feel supported yet challenged. My mentors held me to exacting standards while simultaneously nurturing my growth, a delicate balance that fueled my leadership journey. As I took on leadership roles, I sought to replicate that approach by pushing others to grow while ensuring they felt valued. The impact of mentorship is exponential: when leaders invest in others, the effect ripples through entire teams and organizations. This principle has guided my approach, from military ranks to the corridors of corporate leadership.

Building Williams Leadership Consulting Purpose-Driven Leadership

After retiring from the Army and transitioning into the corporate world, I realized my true purpose: helping leaders and organizations become their best. This epiphany led to the creation of **Williams Leadership Consulting**; an entity focused on more than just profit margins. Its goal is to create lasting impact through a leadership model grounded in purpose.

Shifting from the Army to corporate environments had its challenges, yet it gave me a fresh perspective on leadership gaps. I saw how many organizations lacked a people-centered approach. Thus, the vision for Williams Leadership Consulting was born to empower leaders to discover their "why" and run their organizations with genuine intent. Through coaching, training, and speaking engagements, we spark transformation, challenging leaders to find deeper meaning in their roles and to guide their teams with authenticity.

The Power of Purpose
Inspiring Others to Lead with Meaning

Over the course of my career, I've come to understand that the most effective leaders are those who grasp their purpose. Leadership transcends task management; it's about motivating others with a clear vision and leading from a place of meaning. My mission is to help others uncover that purpose within themselves and equip them with the right tools to lead with honesty and drive.

Purpose propels leaders to exceed expectations, remain resilient in adversity, and energize their teams. Whether in the military, corporate boardrooms, or as the CEO of Williams Leadership Consulting, I've seen firsthand the transformative strength of purpose-driven leadership. When leaders identify their "why," they can confront challenges head-on, inspire others, and leave a meaningful legacy. This is my ultimate pursuit: to help people embrace their purpose, live it courageously, and lead with unwavering authenticity.

My experiences in Jamaica and the United States continue to inform my leadership approach. Every difficulty carried a lesson. Each hardship, a steppingstone to growth. Whether mentoring veterans, advising corporate teams, or speaking to audiences, I strive to encourage leadership rooted in purpose and resilience.

Conclusion
Leading with Integrity, Resilience, and Purpose

My story, from a barefoot boy in the Jamaican countryside to a Command Sergeant Major in the U.S. Army and founder of Williams Leadership Consulting, demonstrates what can be achieved through resilience, integrity, and purpose. Through every stage, I've learned that leadership goes beyond titles; it's a profound duty to lift and empower others. Investing in people, maintaining accountability, and leading with resolve creates a domino effect that inspires others to do the same.

Leadership is an ongoing journey of self-awareness and growth. It demands recognizing both your strengths and weaknesses and always striving to improve. It's not about barking orders but offering an example of what's possible through hard work, compassion, and sincerity. Reflecting on my path from that Jamaican hut to present-day leadership fills me with gratitude for the influence I've always had. Yet the greatest satisfaction comes from knowing this journey continues. I'm committed to guiding others toward their "why" and encouraging them to lead with determination, empathy, and unshakable purpose.

Ready to discover your true "why" and lead with purpose?

Let's connect.
Website: www.williams-leadership.com

LinkedIn: https://www.linkedin.com/in/algrishwilliams

LaShonda Prim

LaShonda Prim is a transformational speaker, author, entrepreneur, and storytelling genius. She is the founder of **Dazzling Divas Empowering Women Toward Success**, whose mission is to **Motivate women to Overcome obstacles, Vision success, and Embrace change** (M.O.V.E.). Her powerful messages stem from her life experiences and challenges, offering relatable and inspiring content for women everywhere.

Born and raised in downtown Charleston, South Carolina, LaShonda lives in Duncan, South Carolina. She is the mother of seven children and is married to Aswad Prim. After serving five years in the U.S. Army as a Unit Supply Specialist and another five years as a Department of Defense civilian, LaShonda resigned from federal service to pursue her calling: motivating and empowering women and young girls to move confidently toward their dreams.

A trained cosmetologist, she now serves as CEO and owner of **Dream Essentials by LaShonda Renee'**, an all-natural skin and body care line, and **Empire Nutrition**, a health and wellness company. LaShonda holds an Associate of Arts in Business Management and a Bachelor of Arts in Business Administration (Entrepreneurship concentration). She co-authored the best-selling collaborative book *Moments in Her Story, Part 2*, and has published two personal works: *Journey Through the Eyes of a Teen Mom* (July 2016) and *Transformed by Grace* (December 2022). Her most recent venture is the creation of "Slay the Day" journals, designed to help girls express themselves, develop vision, and set goals. Guided by her philosophy, "Let everything you do be done with integrity, in love, and excellence." LaShonda continues to champion the transformation of women's mindsets worldwide.

Accomplishments & Involvement

- **Best-Selling Author**
- **Board Member & Director of Mentoring**, Leadership Ladies of the Upstate
- **Board Member, Workshop Host, Panelist, and Emcee** for Girls Who Brunch Tour (Charleston & Greenville/Spartanburg, SC)
- **Mentor** in Spartanburg 5 School District
- **Founder** of Operation Holiday (Adopt a Family) and Single Mothers Holiday Retreat
- **Organizer** of "New Attitude, New Year, New Youth" Explosion, "What's Your Vision" Vision Board Party, and Single Winning on Purpose Conference
- **Radio Appearances** on Kingdom Girls XM Radio Show and XM "Those to Watch" Radio Show
- **Team Building & Confidence Coach** for Burke High School Lady Bulldogs Basketball Team

- **Board Member** for Mothers Against Violence
- **Charleston, SC Ambassador** for Kingdom Girls Tour

Website: https://www.lashondaprim.com/

Chapter 13: The Power to M.O.V.E.: From Being to Becoming

By LaShonda Prim

I decided long ago that I would become a beacon of resilience, inspiration, and transformation in a world hungry for hope and empowerment. Throughout my life, I have traveled many different roads and taken many risks, never afraid to make a move. In every job, task, or accomplishment, my goal has been to uplift others by ensuring they leave my space in a better condition than when they arrived. People often ask me what inspired me to choose a mindset of motivating and inspiring others. My answer is always the same: "Let me take you on a journey called 'The Power of MOVE.'"

Seeds of Purpose

Since my teenage years, I hated seeing anyone upset or sad. I'd do whatever I could to bring a smile to the faces of people I loved. Little did I know that those gestures of kindness—those seeds I planted as a child—were preparing me for my true purpose: **M**otivating women to **O**vercome obstacles, **V**ision success, and **E**mbrace change (M.O.V.E.).

At just 16, I fell deeply in love for the first time. The excitement, the rush, and the decision to share my body with someone I believed I loved led to pregnancy. I remember thinking, *Who can I tell?* I was a senior in high school, involved in JROTC and chorus, holding leadership positions. I was terrified of hearing those dreaded words, *"I'm so disappointed in you."* Despite the fear and judgment, I refused to let circumstances define me. Instead, I decided to channel my energy into a better future: I pursued cosmetology and then enlisted in the military.

A Medical Discharge and the Road to Resilience

My journey as a U.S. Army soldier began enthusiastically, but within the first three weeks of training, I experienced mysterious blackouts when standing too long, running, or even getting out of bed. Soon, I was diagnosed with **Vasovagal Syncope**, a condition where my nervous system overreacts to stress or anger, causing my heart rate and blood pressure to drop and me to faint.

Suddenly, my military career ended after just four years and seven months. Being discharged felt like a failure; my plans and dreams seemed to crumble before my eyes. I thought losing my uniform was the ultimate defeat. Yet, looking back, I realize it was another seed God planted in me, shaping me into the woman He intended me to be rather than who I was trying to become.

Divorce, Motherhood, and Finding Myself Again

Being a mother, a wife, and career-focused was already tough. But my world turned upside down when I faced divorce, a medical discharge, and found myself a single mother of three. I felt alone and unaccomplished, but I still yearned for a better life.

Marriage, which I believed was a sacred bond between a man, a woman, and God, turned into something foreign. I often felt worthless, unwanted, and unloved. Infidelity became a pattern, and I concluded this was simply how our marriage worked. As the pain grew, my anger pushed me to retaliate with my own mistakes; mistakes that made me feel even lower and unworthy.

The breaking point came in an explosive, domestic violence encounter. The pain in that moment, physical, emotional, and spiritual was the final straw. I realized that to find true peace and to heal, I had to become a better version of myself. That was my turning point. That *version* of me which was once sad, depressed, angry, and unmotivated, had to go, and a new chapter needed to begin.

Reconnecting with God's Grace

After a series of broken relationships and heartbreak, I surrendered my life to Jesus Christ. During that time, I recalled a vivid dream: I was joyriding with my siblings, and we got separated in a huge parking lot filled with zombies. Terrified, I felt trapped until a mysterious elderly woman put a medallion around my neck, telling me I was protected as long as I wore it.

That dream showed me God's grace in my life. Each time I thought the enemy had me cornered, God provided an escape. Though I was prideful and disobedient to my calling, He allowed me to go on a journey that lasted over a decade in the making, to understand that He was always protecting me. What seemed like curses turned out to be blessings in disguise, guiding me toward the woman I was meant to be.

Many believe being single and saved is a lonely curse, but for me, it was a chance to find out who I really was in Christ. I learned that to know someone else, I first had to know myself but, to truly know myself, I had to pursue a relationship with God. If your heart is focused on pleasing God, you can better identify the right people and opportunities that align with your purpose.

Chasing a Dream and Choosing Obedience

In 2014, life brought setbacks and blessings. I finally landed a dream job at a major military organization, an opportunity I'd been waiting on for five years. Yet before I accepted, God had given me an assignment: share my story with young women. I founded an organization called **Dazzling Divas**, whose vision was to help women **M.O.V.E.**: *Motivate, Overcome Obstacles, Vision Success, and Embrace Change*. Excited about my new career, I nearly forgot about God's calling.

The stress of maintaining that job soon became overwhelming. One day, I found myself in my car, crying uncontrollably, dreading the thought of going to work, *ever again.* This time, I remembered God's vision for me. I resigned, trusting His plan, even though it didn't come with the financial security I was used to. I dove into my walk as an author and speaker, determined to spread my message. It didn't pay the bills like my old job, but my peace of mind was priceless. My obedience led to my first published book and allowed me to mentor young women in my old high school and church. By transforming each personal battle into a solution, I found a sense of fulfillment that money could never buy.

Entrepreneurship, Trials, and Trusting God

Launching my own ventures was an act of faith. At one point, I couldn't even afford deodorant for my son. My home was in foreclosure, my car was repossessed, and I was barely surviving. Pride almost destroyed me, but God reminded me that *He* is the ultimate provider. Through creativity (and YouTube tutorials!), I learned to make natural deodorant, toothpaste, shampoo, and more. Out of that season of desperation, **Dream Essentials**, my all-natural skin and body care line, was born. Today, those products have been sold throughout the United States and in Europe, which is proof of what happens when you choose to follow God's lead and refuse to give up.

Overcoming Emotional Insecurity

I recently discovered I was harboring emotional insecurities including fears of rejection, failure, and judgment that kept me striving to prove myself worthy. I spent years trying to convince others I was good enough, beautiful, and successful. But no amount of achievement silenced the critics. Eventually, I realized my personal relationship with God needed to grow stronger. The only validation I needed was *His,* not the world's. Once I aligned my focus with God's plan for me, I found lasting peace.

I am now happily married and living the life I once only dreamed about. Understanding that achievements alone won't stop gossip or criticism has freed me. I can use others' negativity as fuel to become a creator by building wealth in mind, body, and spirit, and teaching others to do the same. We all have past traumas and bad experiences, but we can conquer insecurities the same way we overcome any temptation of the flesh: by trusting God's plan above our own desires. When you walk in your calling, your cup runs over to those around you.

Continuing to MOVE Forward

I will always stand by my commitment to M.O.V.E.: *Motivate women to Overcome obstacles, Vision success, and Embrace change.* It's fine to simply *be* who you are, but the true journey is to *become* the person God has destined you to be. That transformation is where real fulfillment and success lie and it is your Super Power.

So, I encourage you to ask yourself:

1. **Are you content with who you are right now?**
2. **Or do you want to meet the person you're meant to become?**

Remember, achieving any dream is possible when you let God take the lead. And no matter what you lose along the way either money, friendships, relationships, or pride. God replaces it with peace, purpose, and true freedom. Embrace the power of MOVE and watch how your life unfolds into something beyond your wildest imagination.

Ready to **M.O.V.E.** connect with me:

https://www.lashondaprim.com/

Dawn Love

Dawn Love is a Certified Personal Development Coach, Author, and Speaker, Dawn is dedicated to serving ambitious divorced women with children. She empowers them to overcome challenges, embrace their strengths, and reclaim their independence. She supports these remarkable women in building financial wealth, nurturing their children with love and grace, and fostering a community where they can thrive and support each other.

Chapter 14: Leading with Grace as a Single Mom Visionary

Dawn Love

Being a single mom sometimes feels like walking on a tightrope while juggling a bag of groceries in one hand and a wiggly puppy in the other. Instead of groceries and puppies, though, the daily load consists of dreams and responsibilities. Despite the chaos, these challenges have taught me to be strong and resourceful and to laugh when life gets overwhelming because, let's be honest, if we didn't laugh, we'd be crying into our coffee every morning.

There's a quote by **Meg Lowrey** that always resonates with me:

"Being a single parent is not a life full of struggles, but a journey for the strong."

She's absolutely right. It's not just about surviving; it's about thriving. I remember a time when my kids asked, "Mom, why do you always have so many things going on?" My answer was simple: "Because I want to show you that we can do anything, even when it feels like we have the weight of the world on our shoulders."

Yet another truth I've learned: Being a single mom doesn't disqualify you from success. **Yvonne Kaloki** said it perfectly:

"Just because I am a single mother doesn't mean I cannot be a success."

That's the guiding principle behind everything I do, and it's what I want to share with you. If you've ever felt like your story is too messy or your schedule too busy, remember that your challenges don't disqualify you, they prepare you.

This chapter is my love letter to single mothers. It's for the moms who stay up late building dreams after the kids go to bed. It's for those who wipe away tears in the car before arriving at basketball games or ROTC competitions, determined to show up with a smile. You are strong, you are capable, and you are called to something bigger than you can imagine.

So, buckle up. We're going to explore how the wild, beautiful, messy journey of single motherhood doesn't just prepare you for leadership, it *calls* you to it. Together, we'll learn how to embrace our stories, lean into our strengths, and lead with grace, vision, and a dash of humor. Because, honestly, what's leadership without a good laugh now and then?

Empowering Lives Through Purpose

Let me ask you a question: Have you ever stared at a mountain of laundry and thought, *"There's got to be more to life than this"*? I know that feeling well. And while the laundry still needs to get done, I realized early on that my purpose was bigger than the day-to-day grind.

My journey hasn't been easy. I've faced severe financial hardships, filed for bankruptcy, and lost my home to foreclosure. I also endured a divorce that affected me mentally, physically, and emotionally, all while battling childhood trauma that left deep emotional scars. On top of that, mental health struggles like depression, anxiety, and panic attacks often made daily life feel impossible.

Through all of it, I've tried to be present for my three sons, but there were times when I was emotionally unavailable because I was busy fighting my own demons. Still, something inside me refused to give up. I fought through the darkness, determined to rebuild for myself and my boys.

While raising three sons, working full-time, and trying to heal, I made the decision to go back to school. It wasn't easy, but sheer determination fueled me. I earned first my bachelor's degree, then my master's, without missing a single extracurricular event for my children, often writing papers at 2 a.m. and catching my breath between their track meets and school plays.

So, what do I do now? I've taken these experiences, the pain, perseverance, and triumph, and used them to help others. Today, I am a coach, speaker, and mentor, working with women to transform their pain into purpose. I offer faith-based coaching programs that guide single moms and other women through major life transitions. Through workshops, group sessions, and one-on-one mentoring, I empower women to reclaim their independence and thrive.

I also authored *Embracing Change: Trusting God Through the Transitions of Life*, a book that serves as a beacon of hope for those navigating trying seasons. Beyond that, I lead conferences designed to inspire growth and equip attendees with tools to embrace their unique paths.

I've had the honor of walking alongside women as they rediscover their worth, start businesses, go back to school, or simply learn to believe in themselves again. It's not about giving them answers, it's about showing them the strength they already possess.

Lessons from the Entrepreneurial Trenches

Running a business is a lot like parenting. Some days, you feel like you have everything under control, meals prepped, kids happy, and deadlines met. Other days, you're wearing mismatched socks and hoping no one notices.

My entrepreneurial journey began with a simple dream: **to make a difference.** But dreams don't pay bills, nor do they come with a handbook. I've learned plenty of lessons the hard way, like the time I tried to do it all, run two businesses, coach clients, and still be Supermom. Spoiler alert: Supermom doesn't exist. But real moms? We show up, even when it's hard.

One of the toughest lessons I learned is that *failure isn't the enemy*. I have failed countless times, launching ideas that never took off, making choices that blew up in my face, and having those moments where quitting seemed easier than pressing on. But here's the secret: failure is just a teacher in an ugly outfit. It doesn't look good, and it doesn't feel good, but it shows you what works and what doesn't.

I've also discovered the power of asking for help. As single moms, we often try to be everything to everyone. But whether in business or life, you can't do it alone. Whether it's assembling a supportive team, leaning on friends, or finding a mentor like Dr. Tabatha Rusell, asking for help is not a sign of weakness, it's a smart strategy.

Then there's balance. Let me tell you a secret: *balance is a myth*. There will always be trade-offs. But if you focus on what truly matters, your family, faith, and purpose, the rest finds a way of falling into place. It's never perfect, but it's authentic. And authenticity is enough.

So, if you stand on the cusp of a new dream, uncertain about taking that leap, let me be your cheerleader. Yes, it's daunting and messy. But it's also utterly worth it. Your story, every struggle and victory, is part of a larger masterpiece you're creating. And trust me, it's going to be beautiful.

My Personal Strategy for Visionary Leadership

I once believed that being a leader meant having all the answers. Over time, I realized true leadership is less about knowing everything and more about consistently showing up. My leadership approach is deeply personal rooted in faith, resilience, and the life lessons I've accumulated.

1. **Vision.** Not just a sticky note on the mirror, but a deep, soul-level vision. I ask myself, *"What do I want this to look like in five or ten years?"* Then I break that vision into actionable steps that fit my often-unpredictable life as a single mom.
2. **Authenticity.** The world is saturated with people pretending to be what they're not. Authenticity acknowledging my fears, failures, and even my flaws, lets others see who I am. Leading from a place of honesty forges meaningful connections and inspires others to embrace their own truths.
3. **Community.** Leadership isn't about standing on a pedestal; it's about lifting others up. I focus on building relationships that empower everyone involved, whether that's mentoring another mom or creating collaborative opportunities.

4. **Faith.** This is the bedrock of my entire strategy. When I reach the end of my rope, my faith reminds me I'm not alone. I pray over my goals, trust the process, and rely on God's guidance when things get murky. This isn't just part of my strategy, it's my foundation.

If you need a blueprint for leadership, that's it: dream big, stay true to yourself, surround yourself with genuine supporters, and believe you're exactly where you need to be. Leadership isn't about perfection; it's about having the persistence and purpose to do what you're called to do. If I can do it, you can too.

Becoming a Visionary Leader of Purpose

Leadership isn't a destination, it's a lifelong journey filled with twists, turns, and unexpected challenges. Every step, every hurdle, and every triumph is part of the process.

When I look back, it's not the titles I've held or the accolades I've earned that matter most. What stands out are the moments of growth, the people I've impacted, and the enduring faith that carried me through. Leadership is about showing up as your best self, one day at a time.

So, if you're standing on the starting line, wondering if you have what it takes, trust me, you do. You've already proven your strength, resilience, and commitment. Now it's time to take the next step.

Let's connect:

- **Visit my website at www.justdawnlove.com**
- Follow me on social media
- Schedule a one-on-one session

Together, we can turn your obstacles into opportunities for a more purposeful future. Remember, leadership isn't about being flawless, it's about growth, perseverance, and the courage to lift others in the process. Your story, messy parts included, can inspire someone else and pave the way for their success.

As you step into your role as a visionary leader, always remember: **You are capable, you are called, and you are enough.** Lead with grace, purpose, and a sprinkle of laughter, because the world needs the unique gifts that only *you* can provide. Trust me, it's going to be extraordinary.

Conclusion

As we conclude this journey through the strategies, insights, and stories of some of the most influential CEOs, one thing becomes abundantly clear: leadership rooted in purpose is a force multiplier. The leaders featured in this book didn't achieve success by accident or by following a standard blueprint. They forged their own paths, guided by vision, resilience, and an unshakable commitment to making an impact.

The principles and strategies shared in these pages are more than tools for organizational success—they are a call to action for leaders everywhere. They challenge us to think beyond profit margins, to focus on people, and to make decisions that reflect not just what's good for the business but what's right for the world. Visionary leadership is about seeing possibilities where others see limitations and having the courage to turn those possibilities into reality.

As you close this book, take a moment to reflect on your own journey as a leader. What is the legacy you want to leave? What values will define your leadership? How will you align your vision with your purpose to create a meaningful impact? These are not questions to be answered lightly, but they are the questions that every leader must face to truly stand out as an extraordinary visionary.

Remember, leadership is not a destination; it's a continuous process of growth, learning, and evolution. The strategies shared by these legendary CEOs are not meant to be copied but they are meant to inspire you to create your own playbook, one that is authentic to your values, strengths, and aspirations.

Your opportunity to lead with purpose starts now. Whether you're managing a team of five or an enterprise of thousands, your ability to inspire, innovate, and impact lives depends on the clarity of your vision and the strength of your conviction. The world needs leaders who aren't afraid to take risks, break boundaries, and prioritize purpose over short-term gain.

As you go forward, may this book serve as a resource, a guide, and a reminder of what's possible when leaders lead with purpose. You have the tools. You have a vision. Now it's time to make your mark.

To the visionaries, the risk-takers, and the purpose-driven leaders, your journey is just beginning. Lead boldly, and lead with purpose.

Thank you for joining us on this journey. Together, we can shape a future where leadership isn't just about success but about significance.

Here's to your success as a Visionary Leader of Purpose.

Published by:

Legacy Pioneers Publishing

Columbia, SC

https://drtabatharussell.com/legacypioneerspublishing

Writing Collaborator:

Lsrobins@yahoo.com

Made in the USA
Middletown, DE
01 February 2025